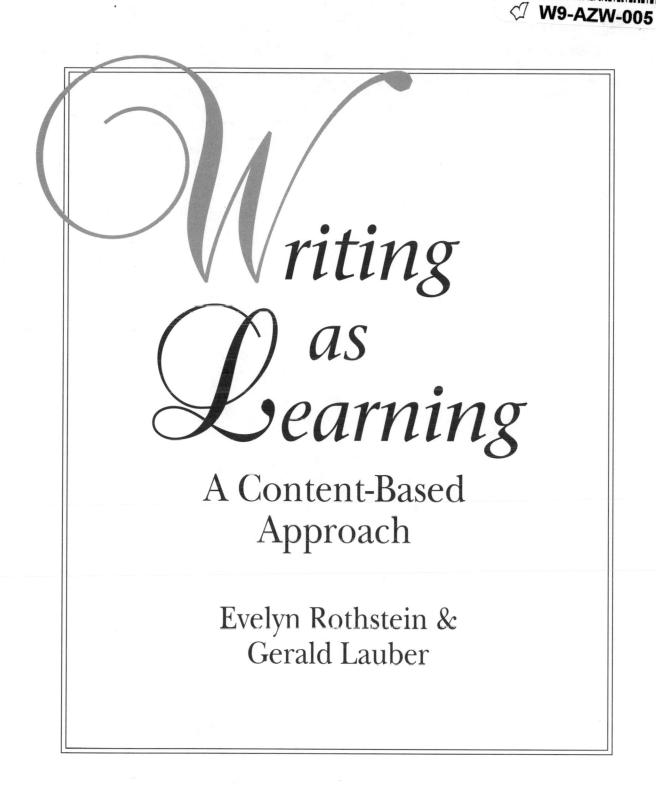

Writing as Learning

A Content-Based Approach

Evelyn Rothstein &
Gerald Lauber

CORWIN PRESS
A SAGE Publications Company
Thousand Oaks, California

For information:

Corwin Press
A Sage Publications Company
2455 Teller Road
Thousand Oaks, California 91320
www.corwinpress.com

Sage Publications Ltd.
1 Oliver's Yard
55 City Road
London EC1Y 1SP
United Kingdom

Sage Publications India Pvt. Ltd.
B-42, Panchsheel Enclave
New Delhi 110 017   India

Printed in the United States of America

ISBN 1-5751-7259-3
LCCN: 00-131464

This book is printed on acid-free paper.

05   06   07   08   09   10   9   8   7   6   5   4   3   2   1

Contents

Preface

*The most important method of education . . .
always has consisted of that in which the pupil
was urged to actual performance.*

Albert Einstein (*Ideas and Opinions* 1954, 60)

Schools across the country have finally acknowledged that learning to write is not merely another subject to be added to an already swollen curriculum but is the "subject" that represents and confirms a student's knowledge, thinking, and in the words of Einstein, "actual performance" (1954, 60). David Perkins (1992) points out the three essential goals of a school: retention of knowledge, understanding of knowledge, and active use of knowledge. With these three goals, students might be expected to remember facts and concepts, relate these facts and concepts to others, and then actively use or apply them in new and possibly creative ways. In a literate culture, writing indisputably becomes the most effective medium for remembering what we must know, for explaining what we already know, and for recording this knowledge for others. This last part is what Perkins considers the core function of knowledge—"passing [it] from one generation to the next" (1992, 5).

Yet learning to write, or the obverse, *teaching* students to write, is often a haphazard enterprise in many schools. When we ask teachers in our workshops, including newly entering teachers still in their early twenties, if they had systematic writing instruction from elementary through high school, few raise their hands. More recent college graduates have heard about or know something about the writing process and recall "having to write" but rarely can they recall learning specific strategies, practiced frequently and consistently, from grade to grade and "across the curriculum." Yet, a school curriculum that puts teaching writing on the back burner or "saves it" for special subjects such as English or language arts offers its students, at best, what Perkins has labeled "inert knowledge— that which students may remember for short-answer tests, but which they cannot use in 'open-ended situations of need, such as writing an essay'" and hardly fits Einstein's concept of education as performance (1992, 22).

The case for *teaching* writing is further strengthened by the expanded understanding of multiple intelligences documented convincingly by Gardner and his colleagues (1983, 1993). By accepting Gardner's definition of intelligence—"the ability to solve problems or to fashion products that are valued in one or more cultural or community settings"—we stop requiring our students to spend hours circling, underlining, and filling in blanks, robbing them of their time and energy to "fashion products," one of which is the written product (Gardner 1983, 7).

Concurring with Perkins's general concept of knowledge, Gardner, in defining *linguistic* intelligence, breaks it down into several aspects, which can only fully blossom in students who are taught and learn to write. First, Gardner speaks of rhetorical ability, which allows persons to persuade or convince others to follow a course of action. In school, this rhetorical ability is developed through public speaking and researched essay writing. A second route to linguistic knowledge is through the "mnemonic capacity," the mind's ability to remember information (Gardner 1993, 92). Students who are taught how to develop and maintain organized lists on specific topics (which we call *Taxonomies*) get an essential tool for learning how to store and retrieve vast amounts of data lodged in their brain.

In addition, linguistic knowledge expands through explanation, which those of us who studied French remember as *explication des textes*. Only the most gifted student writers can develop the skills of explanatory writing without direct teaching. Yet, many students often are asked to write essays such as "Explain the reasons for the Civil War" or "Define religion in at least 200 words" without having had intensive, well-developed instruction in this type of writing. Fourth, Gardner refers to linguistic knowledge arising from one's ability to explain language itself. This is the ability used by writers who not only write linguistic and metalinguistic treatises, but is also used by writers who engage in word play, alliteration, puns and palindromes, and, above all, poetry. While many teachers give attention to these aspects of writing, mainly because they're "light and lively," only a few teachers have learned how to teach their students about the fun of writing about words.

What do we mean by teaching writing? We begin by recognizing that a writer needs *to be or become fluent and organized*. Everyone who writes must have a combination of the appropriate words with the ability to organize those words into meaningful structures. Furthermore, meaning is greatly influenced by the who—how the writer perceives his or her audience. With this concept of fluency plus organization as basic to writing, we develop and teach *specific strategies* that enhance fluency and organization to enable students to write in a broad variety of genres and for a wide range of audiences. The strategies outlined in this book represent a system for teaching students how to write in the four aspects outlined by Gardner, address different audiences, and "fashion products" that meet our culture's needs and standards.

In addition, teaching writing goes beyond helping the student acquire knowledge and producing a worthwhile product. Through the teaching of the process of writing, students learn to select, organize, interrelate, and make connections. Through writing, students develop lexical and syntactic understanding. And now, with the computer as a significant tool and companion, students can use formatting and graphic skills in producing and presenting their written work. Through the teaching of writing, we have the opportunity to develop the characteristics of intelligent behavior that Arthur Costa (1991) has so clearly outlined and detailed. Persistence, perseverance, curiosity, wonderment, metacognition, empathy, and flexibility are not only general intelligent behaviors but are the necessary qualities for good writing and *are the qualities that writing develops*.

The work of Reuven Feuerstein (1997) on *Feuerstein's Instrumental Enrichment and Mediated Learning*, while not focusing specifically on writing, offers another rationale for the value of teaching writing as a mediated learning experience. For generations past, teachers have used the "collect and correct" method of writing of assigning a topic, collecting the papers on the topic, correcting the papers, and returning the papers with editor's marks, be they welcome or unwelcome comments, and giving a grade. However, if we are *teaching writing*, we also are teaching editing, a mediated skill that in the words of Feuerstein requires the teacher to "interpose himself or herself intentionally and systematically" between the student writer and the writing itself (1997, 58). We call this mediated approach "stand-up editing," where the teacher, in line with Feuerstein's approach, prompts and responds to student reflections without judgment and shows the student how to develop and use alternate ideas (e.g., word choices, sentence arrangements, punctuation markers, and so forth).

By continuous learning through writing, the student does not fall into the pit of what Perkins so descriptively calls "fragile knowledge," the superficial learning that teachers ask students to remember for short-answer or standardized tests (1992, 25). To achieve a writing program that teaches students to learn deeply, meaningfully, intelligently, and actively, we have the following recommendations.

First, teachers must conceive of writing as a curriculum unifier. Writing draws together multiple subjects and helps the students understand the unity or interrelatedness of subject matter. In the mathematics class, students write about problems that economists or geographers or historians face. In the English or language arts class, students write with the words of the mathematician, the geographer, or the athlete. Writing is not a separate subject. It is part of all subjects.

To make writing a curriculum unifier, teachers must work to implement a systematic approach to teaching writing to every student in every grade by every teacher and for all the years that a student is in school. Educators certainly wouldn't dream of teaching mathematics every other year or on Thursday afternoon if time permits and without any sequential plan. Why might they think this system is good enough for teaching writing?

For the past twenty years both of us have been involved in the implementation of a systematic writing program with writing as the curriculum unifier. One of us as been in the administration seat, the other has been the trainer. Together, we have seen the outstanding results in student learning, results that are "total." The students who have been taught to write and use writing to learn not only write better, they read better. *(Do you know a good writer who can't read?)* They organize better. (*Good writing is organized writing.*) They have a more enriched vocabulary. (*Writers need words and know where and how to get them.*) They "say" what they mean. (*Good writing is clear, simple, and grammatically appropriate.*)

We offer this book from our experiences as administrator and teacher trainer. We hope that our beliefs, methods, and ideas enrich your students' lives as learners and writers. If we can make this happen, we have given to others a lifelong gift.

EVELYN ROTHSTEIN AND GERALD LAUBER

Introduction

THE IMPORTANCE OF SYSTEMATIC, DEVELOPMENTAL, WRITING INSTRUCTION

Imagine students who have been taught to write systematically and developmentally from kindergarten through twelfth grade. Each year, they have created their own personal thesauruses, written biographical and autobiographical sketches, responded in organized written statements to their growing wealth of knowledge, created their own fables, myths, and folk tales, and expressed their ideas and opinions in personal, persuasive, and explanatory essays and articles. Furthermore, as they created all of this writing, they understood and applied the appropriate conventions of written grammar and spelling.

This utopian dream can be achieved for almost all students when writing becomes the centerpiece of instruction because the ability to write goes hand-in-hand with the ability to use language precisely, creatively, and effectively. Writers are also readers because a writer must have a knowledge base to "say something" worthwhile. Writers feel compelled to enlarge their vocabulary; they soon learn that they must go beyond "a nice day" and "she felt glad."

WHAT THIS BOOK IS ABOUT

This book explains how to implement a systematic plan for teaching writing developmentally and consistently in every subject area and about every subject area. An underlying concept of this book is that students need to learn writing *strategies* that guide them in producing the widest possible range of writing products. By gradually teaching them strategies and then providing practice, students will find their writing voices and writing styles. Students learn to write when they are taught to write and when they are taught to write, they organize, reflect, and clarify.

HOW TO USE THIS BOOK

This book presents twelve specific strategies so that students of all ages can learn how to gather the words they need to write and use the appropriate organizing formats for saying what they need to say. To visualize this approach to teaching writing, the Planning Wheel (see Figure 0.1) illustrates the relation of a subject or topic to the writing strategies. It stands as a visualization of the concept of an integrated approach to teaching any subject area or major topic with the use of specific writing strategies. For example, the circle in the center might represent mathematics or the Thirteen Colonies or animals of the African jungle. Each spoke represents a different writing strategy that may stand alone or be used in combination with other strategies to write about the topic in the circle. In addition, Figure 0.2 shows the learning extensions and writing genres associated with each spoke of the wheel.

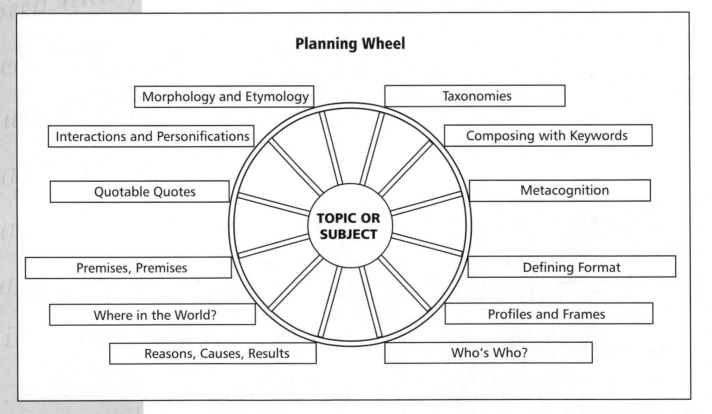

Planning Wheel

Morphology and Etymology

Taxonomies

Interactions and Personifications

Composing with Keywords

Quotable Quotes

Metacognition

TOPIC OR SUBJECT

Premises, Premises

Defining Format

Where in the World?

Profiles and Frames

Reasons, Causes, Results

Who's Who?

Figure 0.1

Strategy and Definition	Learning Extensions	Genres
Taxonomies—Alphabetical lists of terms related to the subject or topic (e.g., algebra, borrow, computation, divide)	• Fluency and organization • Advance organizing • Notetaking • Pre- and post-assessment	• ABC book
Composing with Keywords—Using the words from the taxonomies to compose sentences and paragraphs	• Sentence composing • Paragraphing • Focusing on topic	• Response log • Journal
Metacognition—Self-awareness of knowledge that begins with statements such as "I know that I know; I know that I need to know; I know that I don't know."	• Questioning • Research • Response to learning	• Explanation of factual knowledge • Inquiry into new knowledge
Defining Format—A three-part format to define a term (e.g., What is a triangle?) that consists of the question, the category, and the characteristics	• Questioning • Categorizing • Detailing • Vocabulary building • Paragraph development	• Explanation of factual knowledge • Descriptive writing • Compare and contrast
Frames and Profiles—Templates for outlining information in a broad spectrum of topics and subjects	• Biographic and subject research • Paraphrasing and recreating	• Report • Oral presentation • Reference material
Who's Who—Develops formats for writing about persons of accomplishment or literary characters	• Biographic research • Literary interpretation • Character development	• Autobiography • Biography • Literary analysis • Book review
Reasons, Causes, Results—An organizational essay format for detailing reasons, causes, purposes, results, and procedures	• Outlining • Detailing • Paragraphing • Focusing on topic	• Personal expression • Persuasion • Explanation
Where in the World—Map study and geographic research related to the subject or topic (e.g., *Arab Traders and the Invention of Zero*)	• Geographic and historic research • Map and globe skills • Use of charts and graphics	• Social issues • Geographic and historical issues • Explanatory and factual writing
Premises, Premises—A format for writing literary summaries that serve as the basis for story development	• Organizing essential ideas • Literary structures • Literary understanding	• Fictional format • Play and film • Monologue and dialogue
Quotable Quotes—The development of dialogue by the writer and the response of the reader to the quoted statements of the authors and other writers	• Response to statements, opinions, and ideas • Making inferences • Writing succinctly	• Play and screen writing • Fiction • Social and moral issue
Interactions and Personifications—A writing strategy in which a character or person writes to another character or person on topics or ideas related to the subject area (e.g., *Pythagoras to Hypatia on a Mathematical Issue*)	• Research • Audience and voice • Imagination and creativity • Insight and empathy	• Letters—all formats • Humor • Reality and fantasy
Morphology and Etymology—The study of the formation and history of selected words related to the subject or topic (e.g., add, adds, added, adding, additional, additionally, additive, addendum)	• Grammar • Spelling patterns • Language history	• Alliteration • Word stories • Myths and legends • Poetic forms

Figure 0.2

The strategies are presented in the order in which it is suggested one implements them. However, each strategy is capable of being part of an integrated approach. Perhaps begin by teaching the strategies in the order presented on the Planning Wheel and in the text. By following this arrangement one helps students develop *vocabulary and use the appropriate genres or format,* the two essential requirements for learning to write. For example, the building of *Taxonomies*—lists of words on a topic—provides students with the ideas that they need to begin and develop a story or theme. From these Taxonomies, students create sentences or paragraphs, focusing again on the topic, called *Composing with Keywords,* a strategy especially valuable for factual and research writing.

Writers are definers of ideas, and we have named our third strategy *Defining Format,* which guides students in defining a term by stating the category to which it belongs and then add the qualities or attributes that separate it from other members of that category. A pencil, therefore, is not merely "something to write with," but is a "writing tool" that uses graphite, is made of wood, and so forth. Initially, if you show your students just these three strategies, you will give them the basic tools for becoming fluent and organized.

But, of course, there's more, because students must learn to write in different genres and in a variety of subject areas. The writer is both constructing and solving problems at the same time: "How do I start?" "What should I say?" "Who am I writing to?" "Is this what she/he wants?" "Is it too long?" "Too short?" "What grade will I get?" As students become familiar with the basic strategies and begin to apply them in their journal writing or other written assignments they can move on. When you introduce *Profiles and Frames,* followed by *Who's Who,* the strategy for writing autobiographies, biographies, and character descriptions, you will be carrying forth providing applications and opportunities for using Taxonomies, Keywords, and Defining Format, so that your students never stop practicing previously introduced writing strategies. By developing this accumulation of knowledge about writing, you help your students become effective writers. Students become effective writers by acquiring knowledge about writing and developing their writing skills. Furthermore, throughout the whole writing instructional process, you will be including the concept of writing as *re-vision*—writing as re-writing or re-staging or re-forming. Your students will add to their Taxonomies or recompose their sentences or combine the information on the Defining Format. When your students are ready for Reasons, Causes, Results, you will also be teaching them planning, outlining, layout, and publishing. Every strategy is knowledge-based and extends into other areas of the curriculum. For example, when your students are engaged in studying a piece of literature, they will keep a Taxonomy of terms or characters, use the Defining Format to define specialized meanings, research Where in the World the story takes place, and respond to the quotations stated by the author or the author's characters.

Go slowly in introducing the strategies, making sure the students have extensive practice. This practice will be easy and natural if you make it part of all subject area learning. When you are teaching mathematics or science or social studies, have your students set up Taxonomies, respond to questions with Keywords, define their terms with definition format, express their opinions using Reasons, Causes, Results, and use Interactions and Personifications to write from a new or imaginary point of view.

Chapter 1: "The Elements of Writing as Learning" provides an overview of the elements of writing as learning and defines the purposes of using specific strategies.

Chapter 2: "Building Taxonomies for Fluency" introduces the concept of *Taxonomies*—lists of words pertaining to a specific topic—that provides students with the means for collecting vocabulary, which they can in turn use in their writing. The development and use of the student's Personal Thesaurus is also discussed as a ready reference for would be writers.

Chapter 3: "Composing with Keywords" demonstrates how Taxonomies can be used to develop sentence building skills by employing the Keywords strategy.

Chapter 4: "Metacognition" delves into the recognized need for students to identify and become aware of *what they know what they know.* Self-awareness and reflection upon one's learning prepares students to share their knowledge with others.

Chapter 5 : "Defining Format" shows teachers how to guide students to define a term by stating the category to which it belongs and adding the qualities and characteristics that separate it from other members of the category. The Defining Format strategy aids students greatly in developing fluency and organization in their writing.

Chapter 6: "Profiles and Frames" builds on the strategies introduced in the previous chapters by concentrating on organizational templates that can be used across subject areas. These templates, set up as Profiles (informational guides) or Frames (story or nonfiction outlines) allow teachers to help students structure and organize their writing but also allow for the creativity of students' own words.

Chapter 7: "Who's Who" is devoted to techniques that can be applied to learning and writing about persons. A variation on the Defining Format is introduced called the Biographic Format. Methods for developing student autobiographies are also discussed.

Chapter 8: "Reasons, Causes, Results" introduces the technique students can use to write personal, persuasive, and explanatory essays where students begin their writing with the phrase "There are three reasons why . . ."

Chapter 9: "Where in the World" relates ways students can write and learn about the places that are included in their readings, the geography of a battlefield, or the setting of a story (time and place). This chapter consolidates the previously presented strategies and opens up new vistas in writing.

Chapter 10: "Premises, Premises" provides strategies that help students process their understanding of written material by transforming it into "movie," and thereby helps students visualize what the author had in mind. This is a creative process that requires the students to write in the specialized genres of premise, treatment, scripts, and dialogue.

Chapter 11: "Quotable Quotes" shows ways for students to respond in writing to the words of literary characters and famous (or infamous) people. By writing a personal reaction, students gain a fuller understanding of the various meanings of words in the context of the time, place, and circumstances in which they were delivered.

Chapter 12: "Personifications and Interactions" uses personification—the ascribing of human characteristics to animals or objects. Included are ways that students can write from another point of view. Personification helps make writing as learning vivid and exciting, requiring students to know in-depth who they are when assuming various personae and therefore communicate that understanding to others.

Chapter 13: "Morphology, Etymology, and Grammar" focuses on ways teachers and students alike can examine and analyze the words of their language. When students begin to explore the history of words, they learn not only the meaning of the words but the depth of the word meanings.

Chapter 14: "Writing as Editing" recognizes that writing and editing are not separate exercises, and are a portion of the process of understanding and communicating written information.

Chapter 15: "Active Learning" further illuminates how to use all of the strategies.

In recognition of the significant role that computers now play in the process of writing, a section called "Linking to the Computer" is included at the end of each chapter.

With standards in nearly every state demanding student writing in every subject area, teachers must be able to teach writing as part of content. Students need to know and be able to use subject-area terminology across content areas so that they can fully integrate in their minds the relationship between the subjects. This book provides teachers with concrete and practical ways of bringing this about.

CHAPTER 1

The Elements of Writing as Learning

Strategies, Genres, Topics, and Tools

Writing is a unique form of learning because it allows us to see our thoughts and develop them.

—Colleen Kennedy

STRATEGIES FOR WRITING

Today most schools accept writing as a process in contrast to the older rule-bound, product-oriented approach in which the student writes and the teacher corrects (Kennedy 1996). In a process environment, students are guided through successive, and possibly recursive, steps of prewriting, drafting, revising, editing, and, if possible or appropriate, publishing. This arrangement of steps is probably a good description of what a writer *might* do in the development of a piece of writing, but what is missing are the instructional strategies that guide the student towards the fulfillment of these steps. Some questions are central to this process. What is prewriting? Does it mean discussion? Research? Interviewing? Outlining? Does the writer actually write anything during *prewriting*? How does a student write a draft, and what are the elements of a good draft so that it becomes an excellent final product? What steps of the writing process does the student have to practice? Expansion of ideas? Use of transitional words? Reduction of clutter? And above all, what does the teacher teach students so that students can write with the voice of those who are called writers? Essentially, the teacher teaches writing with writing so that writing becomes "a part of an integrated comprehensive set of activities used to enhance student learning" (VanTassel-Baska 1996, 144).

One way to think of writing is as a way of generating meaning through *fluency plus organization*. Simply put, a writer needs the words and the

taxonomies

composing with keywords

metacognition

defining format

profiles and frames

who's who?

reasons, causes, results

where in the world

premises, premises

quotable quotes

personifications and interactions

morphology, etymology, and grammar

organizational structures that make the words convey the writer's ideas or message through development and coherence (Spivey 1996). With this concept of writing, different writing strategies build fluency for the topic or content and provide the students with an organizational schema for writing specific genres to various audiences. As the students learn and practice a strategy, they use and integrate one or more of the writing process procedures, which are likely to include prewriting, planning, drafting, and revising. In addition, students become aware that "writing is the process of selecting as well as organizing" (Spivey 1996, 38) and that a good piece of writing generates meaning that "has organization, development, and coherence" (Spivey 1996, 41).

The strategies described in this book can be used to teach students how to write for all aspects of the curriculum. Primary grade and special needs students may only be ready for a few of the strategies, and throughout this book, those strategies applicable to them are noted.

THE GENRES OF WRITING

All writing of consequence has what is called *genre,* or form that follows a recognizable organizational scheme. A genre refers to a specific, definable type of writing (or art) with noticeable attributes. A novel is organized quite differently from a research paper. A haiku is set up differently from a ballad. Writing genres may be fiction, nonfiction, or poetry. Experienced writers learn to mix their genres so that in addition to myth, legend, fairy tale, novel, essay, and so forth, there is biographical fiction, descriptive narrative, and personal essay.

Despite the need for understanding and writing within a genre, many students remain unaware of genre formats and how to write within the parameters of their structures. Many times this lack of awareness results from being assigned writing topics such as "Write an essay about. . . ." that either are too global or that lack format specificity. Such topics cause students to be uncertain as to whether the essay is to be persuasive, explanatory, or personal.

When students are asked to write about a famous person without instruction, they end up creating a piece that strings facts together and is likely to resemble an obituary. Writing assignments that begin with words such as *discuss, tell,* or *describe* often cause students to ramble, digress, or switch voices, changing from objective to personal or vice versa without any reason. Novice writers, therefore, must learn what genres are and how they are structured or organized. Learning about genres is developmental, of course, so that young writers (and probably inexperienced writers) are limited in what they can write. Even at adult levels, few people can write well in a variety of genres. Nevertheless, in a school with a systematic, strategy-based writing program, students can be introduced to writing fables, legends, news reports, plays, and numerous other genre forms.

Following are two lists, or Taxonomies, that contain examples of the types of genres that students can learn to write. One list contains fictional and non-fictional formats, and the other list has different poetry genres. The lists can be used by teachers as planning and organizational tools. Teachers can add other genres to these lists and place checkmarks in the Plan to Teach column to indicate the genres they plan to teach to their students.

TAXONOMY SHEET
Genres—Fiction and Nonfiction

	Genres	Appropriate Grades	Plan to Teach		Genres	Appropriate Grades	Plan to Teach
A	autobiography	3+		L	legend	4+	
	animal story (fiction)	1+			laboratory report	4+	
	animal story (factual)	1+			learning log	1+	
	ABC book	1+		M	mystery	3+	
	adventure story	3+			myth	3+	
B	biography	3+			metacognitive statement	1+	
	business letter	4+		N	novel	7+	
C	comedy skit	5+			narrative	2+	
	character sketch	3+		O	opinion statement	1+	
	comics	3+		P	personal essay	2+	
D	descriptive essay	3+			persuasive essay	3+	
E	explanatory essay	4+			play	3+	
	editorial	5+		Q			
F	fairy tale	2+		R	research report	4+	
	folk tale	2+			recipe	1+	
	friendly letter	1+		S	short story	6+	
G	ghost story	2+			script	3+	
	greeting card	1+			science fiction	4+	
H	humorous story	1+			speech	2+	
	how-to piece	1+		T	travelogue	3+	
	history article	3+			technical report	6+	
I	interview	3+			tall tale	3+	
	instructions	2+		U			
J	jokes	1+		V			
	journal	1+		W	wildlife story	3+	
K				X, Y, Z			

Figure 1.1

TAXONOMY SHEET
Genres—Poetic Forms

	Genres	Appropriate Grades	Plan to Teach
A	acrostic	1+	
B	ballad	3+	
C	couplet	1+	
	cinquain	2+	
D	diamante	2+	
E	epic	4+	
F	free verse	1+	
G			
H	haiku	2+	
I			
J			
K			
L	lyric(s)	4+	
	limerick	3+	
M			
N			
O			
P			
Q	quatrain	3+	
R			
S	sonnet	6+	
T			
U			
V			
W			
X			
Y			
Z			

Figure 1.2

THE WRITING TEACHER AND THE WRITING CLASSROOM

Which teachers are responsible for teaching writing? The language arts teacher? The English teacher? Most teachers are all too familiar with middle school and high school students who challenge the social studies or science teacher who expects correct spelling and appropriate grammar. "Isn't it the job of the English teacher to worry about our spelling and verbs?" they ask. And what about the music, art, and physical education teachers? What is their role in asking students to write? Do they have the time or the skills? And will students accept writing assignments from a gym teacher? Or a music teacher?

In the elementary school, similar issues may arise. If there are pull-out programs—gifted, special education, reading, mathematics—does the "special" teacher teach writing or do these students miss class writing lessons? Hopefully, if writing is taught as a way of learning throughout the school, all students are continuously engaged in both instruction and practice with *all* teachers.

While recognizing that teachers often see themselves as specialists in specific subject areas, writing promotes, develops, organizes, and enhances all learning, and every subject has its own *literature*—from mathematics to sports. Writing defines subject areas, deepening one's knowledge and recall (Kennedy 1996). The sports writer, for example, touches upon statistics, history, geography, health, and character behaviors and values. Therefore, every classroom must reflect students' writings as part of their understanding of and involvement in their learning. As stated by Nancy Atwell, "Writing is basic to thinking about and learning knowledge *in all fields* as well as communicating that knowledge" (1998, xiii).

The first indicators of good instruction throughout a school are the walls. The slogan "The Walls Talk" reflects an active visualization of what students are doing and learning. Commercial posters and signs on the walls tell one story about instruction, while students' writings and projects tell a different story. Educators, parents, and other visitors should be able to walk into a classroom after the students have left and know from the walls whether or not they would want to be in that classroom themselves or would want their own children to be in that classroom. A classroom should be a living panorama where the visitor is invited to comment and marvel at the students' work, especially what students have written about their learning or their insights on their learning. The classroom and hallway walls are the visual representation of what has been taught and *what has been learned.*

With the classroom as a showcase of student accomplishment, all work is displayed aesthetically and invitingly. A simple frame of construction paper and a statement about the work announce the importance of what is being displayed. Following are suggested phrases that serve as both announcements and invitations to writers and observers alike. Many students enjoy creating their own witty or catchy phrases, and teachers can provide opportunities for brainstorming bulletin board captions or encourage student suggestions.

Bulletin Board Invitations for Students' Writing

- Writers Under Construction
- Writers Meet Here
- Author's Column
- Writer's Convention—Stop and Browse
- Mathematicians' Write-Abouts
- Writers Wanted—Space Available
- Writer's Scene
- A World of Writers
- Publisher's Place
- Need a Good Definition? Ask a Writer.
- Powerful Persuasions and Exacting Explanations
- Writers Never Forget
- Need a Friend? Write a Letter.
- Write? Right!
- Write Today. Write Tomorrow. Write Forever.
- We're in the Write Company

A second indicator of good instruction is the easy availability or accessibility of writing tools. Some writers need different kinds of writing paper—yellow pads for drafts and white or special paper for final and published copies. Most writers need and love different kinds of writing implements—well-sharpened, good lead pencils, easy flowing pens, and colored markers. And, of course, there is the computer, with its word processing and graphics programs, and the Internet, each of which are becoming more accessible and user-friendly as tools for writing. Writers also need spell checkers, age-appropriate and unabridged dictionaries, atlases, globes, and reference material.

Of course, not all classrooms or schools are able to provide all of these tools. Yet, think of how difficult writing is without them. Imagine building a house without plans and with only a small hammer and a few nails. Without the necessary tools, writing can be equally as difficult. Figures 1.3 and 1.4 provide suggestions for the basic writing materials needed to support good writing instruction. Adjustments and substitutions will need to be made based upon the available resources and budgetary constraints.

Non-technological Materials to Support Instructional Writing Program—Elementary Grades

- Draft paper—yellow and white pads
- Final copy paper—white lined and unlined
- Publishing paper—colored construction paper
- Writing implements—soft lead pencils, different colored pens, markers
- Spiral notebook(s) for journals, lists, and writing strategy models
- Grade-appropriate dictionaries and thesauri
- Unabridged dictionary (for grades 3 and up)
- Wall of Words, including months, days of the weeks, seasons, colors, animals, names of classmates, mathematical terms, occupations, or whatever is needed for the students' writing
- Wall of Topics
- Story frames and sentence starters
- Charts of editing and proofreading rules
- Labels, sticky notes, glue sticks
- Files of magazines and pictures
- Blank greeting cards and envelopes
- Blank bound books
- Bookbinder and laminator
- Anthologies of nursery rhymes, fairy tales, myths, folk tales, and legends
- Globes and maps

Figure 1.3

MIDDLE SCHOOL AND HIGH SCHOOL

While materials for writing are often the responsibility of middle and high school students, whenever possible schools should supply the basic writing materials needed to provide motivation for writing for publication or presentation to other students. The materials listed in Figure 1.4 are also helpful.

Non-technological Materials to Support Instructional Writing Program—Middle School and High School

- Unabridged dictionary
- Style manuals
- Alphabetical thesaurus and topic thesaurus
- Spell checkers
- Books of word histories and origins
- Globes and maps
- Book of concise biographies
- Appropriate magazines, periodicals, and newspapers

Figure 1.4

What Should I Write About?

William Zinsser has stated that "the only way to write is to force yourself to produce a certain number of words on a regular basis" (1980, 53). To many teachers, this statement, while probably correct, may seem absurd or impossible: "I'm a mathematics teacher with a year's curriculum to cover" or "My students are just learning to read and can barely hold a pencil" and "Zinsser is talking about professional writers, not young students." Yet, one learns to write by writing, just as one learns to bowl by bowling. Following are suggestions to get students to want to engage in the practice of writing.

First, have students create a list (Taxonomy) early in the school year of topics they might write about in class. Obviously, the list will vary depending on whether the class is a second grade class or a chemistry class. Have the students set up the list alphabetically as shown in Figure 1.5 and ask them to brainstorm for topics. Ask students what they think they will learn about and have them turn their answers into topics. A third grader might say, "How to do multiplication." Under M, the student would write "multiplication." In a chemistry class, suggested topics could be "contributions of chemists," "discoverers of elements," "alchemy and chemistry," and "careers in chemistry." Figures 1.5, 1.6, and 1.7 show three samples of lists of topics. Lists of possible writing topics can be generated at the beginning of the year or course and modified, updated, and otherwise revised throughout the year or program.

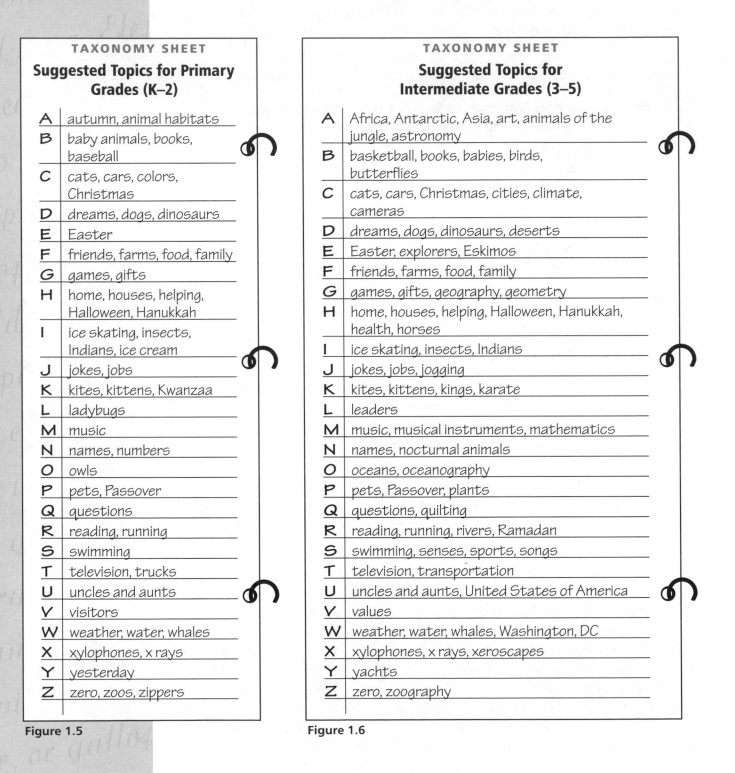

TAXONOMY SHEET

Suggested Topics for Primary Grades (K–2)

A	autumn, animal habitats
B	baby animals, books, baseball
C	cats, cars, colors, Christmas
D	dreams, dogs, dinosaurs
E	Easter
F	friends, farms, food, family
G	games, gifts
H	home, houses, helping, Halloween, Hanukkah
I	ice skating, insects, Indians, ice cream
J	jokes, jobs
K	kites, kittens, Kwanzaa
L	ladybugs
M	music
N	names, numbers
O	owls
P	pets, Passover
Q	questions
R	reading, running
S	swimming
T	television, trucks
U	uncles and aunts
V	visitors
W	weather, water, whales
X	xylophones, x rays
Y	yesterday
Z	zero, zoos, zippers

Figure 1.5

TAXONOMY SHEET

Suggested Topics for Intermediate Grades (3–5)

A	Africa, Antarctic, Asia, art, animals of the jungle, astronomy
B	basketball, books, babies, birds, butterflies
C	cats, cars, Christmas, cities, climate, cameras
D	dreams, dogs, dinosaurs, deserts
E	Easter, explorers, Eskimos
F	friends, farms, food, family
G	games, gifts, geography, geometry
H	home, houses, helping, Halloween, Hanukkah, health, horses
I	ice skating, insects, Indians
J	jokes, jobs, jogging
K	kites, kittens, kings, karate
L	leaders
M	music, musical instruments, mathematics
N	names, nocturnal animals
O	oceans, oceanography
P	pets, Passover, plants
Q	questions, quilting
R	reading, running, rivers, Ramadan
S	swimming, senses, sports, songs
T	television, transportation
U	uncles and aunts, United States of America
V	values
W	weather, water, whales, Washington, DC
X	xylophones, x rays, xeroscapes
Y	yachts
Z	zero, zoography

Figure 1.6

Students also need to know the resources for writing and becoming a writer—tools beyond the encyclopedia and copying articles off the Internet. Figure 1.8 shows a Taxonomy for resources.

TAXONOMY SHEET

Suggested Topics for Chemistry

A | agriculture and chemistry, atoms in our lives
B | blood chemistry
C | chemistry in the news, chemists of accomplishment, chemical warfare
D | DNA in medical treatment, detectives and chemistry, drug abuse
E | elements and their names
F | forensics, food chemistry
G | gold—commodity of greed gold—commodity of medicine
H | history of chemistry
I | inventions of chemists
J | jokes for chemists
K | Krypton—material and birthplace of Superman
L | luminescence in our lives
M | mathematics and chemistry
N | nuclear chemistry
O | osmosis for living
P | plastics—past and future
Q | quinine and the story of malaria
R | radiation and cancer
S | silicones in the news
T | turpentine—home and medicine product
U | uranium and its discovery
V | vitamins for health
W | whiskey—product and history
X | xerography
Y | yeast for the baker
Z | zinc for health

Figure 1.7

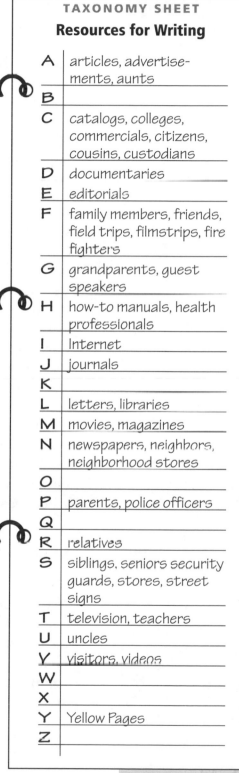

TAXONOMY SHEET

Resources for Writing

A | articles, advertisements, aunts
B |
C | catalogs, colleges, commercials, citizens, cousins, custodians
D | documentaries
E | editorials
F | family members, friends, field trips, filmstrips, fire fighters
G | grandparents, guest speakers
H | how-to manuals, health professionals
I | Internet
J | journals
K |
L | letters, libraries
M | movies, magazines
N | newspapers, neighbors, neighborhood stores
O |
P | parents, police officers
Q |
R | relatives
S | siblings, seniors security guards, stores, street signs
T | television, teachers
U | uncles
V | visitors, videos
W |
X |
Y | Yellow Pages
Z |

Figure 1.8

THE STUDENT AS WRITER AND EDITOR

Perhaps the greatest benefit derived from the shift of the teacher-correction model of writing to the writing process has been the teachers' and (hopefully) students' understanding that a writer is his or her own editor—at least initially. Many persons can probably remember receiving writing assignments that they wrote under duress, either in class or at home, and then handed in what they presumed were finished copies. And, unless they were both gifted writers and mind readers, many got their papers back from their teachers red-inked with uncomplimentary comments on their grammar, spelling, and organization (or lack of). Hopefully, most teachers today have rethought this unpleasant and unhelpful system and see themselves as writing mentors, coaches, and counselors.

In order to facilitate writing and move students from draft to publication, several procedures are essential. First, students need to understand the concept of a draft copy. A draft copy is any initial effort and implies that the writer has done little or no editing. On the other hand, it is not, as some teachers indicate, a "sloppy copy." A draft copy is a work in progress that *temporarily* frees the writer from worrying too much about the conventions of spelling, grammar, and format. It also may free the writer from worrying about appropriate or upgraded word choices so that she or he can just get the essential ideas down. Draft writing also allows the writer to, as Zinsser states, "summon out of the brain some cluster of thoughts or memories" (1980, 57) that previously had not been anticipated. It is important to distinguish between a draft copy and a sloppy copy. Good draft writing results in a well-thought out piece that is organized and ready for improvement. Figure 1.9 provides a sample of the basic guidelines for writing a draft copy given to students at the beginning of the school year.

LINKING TO THE COMPUTER

It is almost impossible to imagine any writer of the future writing by "hand." Although the common writing implements—pens and pencils—may still have a place next to a stationary telephone (another anachronism of the future), today's students will be, at least until the next monumental invention, "computer bound." Hopefully, all schools are providing computers and computer instruction, especially in word processing, graphics, and using the Internet.

As teachers begin their writing programs, it is useful for them, or the computer specialists, to introduce students to what is truly the writer's best friend—the word processor. Although teaching word processing is beyond

---

Guidelines for Writing a Draft Copy

The draft copy is the first of several copies in your writing. After you have written your draft copy, you may go on to revise your draft either by hand or by computer. You might have one or two more revisions before someone else edits it. Then you may be ready for a final or even published copy. The number of copies you write depends on the importance of the piece of writing to you personally, to getting a certain grade, or to being recognized as a good writer. To get started in this writing process, you should begin with the best possible draft you can write. Here are some guidelines to help you.

1. Mark your paper "Draft Copy" so that the reader knows you have a "work in progress."
2. If you are writing by hand, be sure to skip lines on your paper. If you are writing with a computer, set the computer file for double line spacing.
3. Before beginning to write, prepare some "notes," such as a web or cluster, Taxonomy, Defining Format, Profile, Essay outline, Venn diagram, or whatever else you know or your teacher has shown you.
4. Review and keep in mind the guidelines of the assignment: its length, audience, purpose, and any other requirements you are asked to include.
5. If you are writing by hand, cross out your changes and avoid erasing. Erasing interrupts your thinking and keeps you from moving ahead. Remember, you are in draft copy so you don't have to worry too much about neatness.
6. Read your draft copy aloud to anyone willing to listen, keeping a pencil or pen in your hand to make changes.
7. Ask someone you know to read your paper aloud to you. After it is read, make any desired changes as soon as possible.
8. Listen to suggestions for improving your writing and make the changes you agree with. You also might want to get a second opinion on some suggestions.
9. Above all, be patient with yourself and your writing. You will be rewarded with having written great pieces.

Figure 1.9

the scope of this book, introducing some basic word processing skills to students using computers to compose will help them learn to use the computer with ease. Following are skills students should know in order to write using a computer:

- Setting margins
- Line spacing
- Paragraph formatting
- Keyboarding capital and lowercase letters
- Setting font styles and sizes
- Using spelling and grammar checkers
- Using the thesauruses
- Knowing how to highlight, cut, copy, and paste

■ Creating and saving files

■ Printing documents

By being familiar with these computer functions, students will learn to accept writing as a process that moves from draft copy to publication. With mastery of word processing, students will less likely hand in draft copies filled with spelling, grammar, and other errors that require the markings of the teacher's dreaded red pen. And for the teacher, there is the glory (or at least the pleasure) of the reduction of eye strain brought on by unreadable handwriting.

taxonomies

*composing with
keywords*

metacognition

defining format

*profiles
and frames*

who's who?

*reasons, causes,
results*

*where in
the world*

premises, premises

quotable quotes

*personifications
and interactions*

*morphology,
etymology,
and grammar*

CHAPTER 2

Building Taxonomies for Fluency

The ABCs of Word Power

*The Thesaurus is to the writer what a rhyming
dictionary is to the songwriter.*

—William Zinsser

THE GIFT OF WORDS—CREATING TAXONOMIES

Writers need words. And what is most wonderful about words is that *they
are free* and in the public domain. When students find ways to have the
words they need for writing, they have *what* to say. When they realize that
words can be shared and received from others—that people both receive
words and give words—they discover that accumulating words is much
easier than they thought. This belief in the power of having words is the
basis of the first strategy—building Taxonomies.

Taxonomy is used here to refer to a list of words that are related to a specific topic or subject area. A person can build a Taxonomy of terms related to waterways, geometry, or capital cities. The purpose of building
Taxonomies is to provide the writer (student) with the terms or words that
she or he might need for writing about a certain topic.

THE BUILDING OF THE PERSONAL THESAURUS

To make the Taxonomy manageable and organized, it helps to set it up
alphabetically. By using the alphabet as the placeholder for the words, the
students have two major advantages. First, words can easily be found or
retrieved as in any alphabetical system. A second, and very valuable advantage of using the alphabet, is that it pushes or motivates students to search
for words or terms beyond the ordinary or expected. Students often want

to look up words in the dictionary that begin with the letters *Q, X,* and *Z* to complete their Taxonomy. While this completion is not the purpose for the Taxonomy, students nonetheless get the benefit of finding words such as *quiescent, xenophobic,* and *zoography* and then deciding if these words relate to their topic.

As the students build their Taxonomies across the curriculum, they are creating *Personal Thesauruses* that they can add to or refer to on a continuous basis as they acquire knowledge. Beginning in either second or third grade, students should have their own spiral notebooks set up to keep track of the numerous Taxonomies that relate to their subject areas and growing interests. By entering the Taxonomies in a notebook, the students build a *Personal Thesaurus* to which they can refer for words and terms and to which they can add as they learn more about a particular topic or subject. A simple way to set up the notebook is to have the students create a Table of Contents with the Taxonomies listed or dated in the order in which they were started, as illustrated in Figure 2.1.

Taxonomy Table of Contents

Date	Subject	Topic	Page
September 14	Mathematics	Types of Numbers	4
September 26	Science	Rain Forests	6
October 8	Social Studies	Explorers	8
October 15	Holidays	Halloween	10
November 1	Mathematics	Geometry	12
November 10	Social Studies	Colonies & Civilization	14
November 13	Holidays	Thanksgiving	16
December 3	Health	Healthy Foods	18
December 3	Myself	Personal Identities	20

Figure 2.1

In addition to the creation of the personal thesaurus, Taxonomies can be used for the following purposes:

- Advance organizing and assessment of prior knowledge
- Continuous notetaking
- Vocabulary development
- Development and assessment of new knowledge
- Building cooperative learning experiences
- Starting to write

Advance Organizing and Assessment of Prior Knowledge

E. D. Hirsch Jr. stated that "we use past knowledge to interpret (our) window of experience" (1987, 48). In his extensive discussion of the structure of background knowledge and its importance for developing new knowledge, he stresses the essentialness of schemata, or organizational formats to achieve meaningful learning. He pointed out that through schemata, we "store knowledge in retrievable form" and "organize knowledge in more and more efficient ways so that it can be applied rapidly and efficiently" (1987, 56). He further stated that one's personal background knowledge allows for the understanding and communication through spoken and written language.

Teachers are certainly aware of this schematic principle or concept, yet may not always have efficient means for assessing what their students know about a given topic *before* they introduce the topic. One way to assess background or prior knowledge might be to give a pretest, but this can be cumbersome and time-consuming, especially for young students. The Taxonomy, as a pre-assessment tool, can serve effectively as the advance organizer that provides a window for glimpsing what students individually and collectively already know about what educators want them to know.

Students set up their Taxonomies in an ABC format, as shown in chapter 1. Teachers working with early primary grades may want to make a form for the students' use in advance and also have a poster-size version available. The teacher introduces the Taxonomy by telling the students they will be starting a new topic (e.g., deserts) and she or he would like to know what words they already know about the topic. The teacher can either write the words for the students on his or her own chart or ask each student to write his or her own words, working alone (solo) at first. While observing the students as they write their words, the teacher is able to assess the students' prior knowledge of the topic. Following a brief period in which students enter words on the Taxonomy, the teacher asks the students to contribute the words they have entered and, possibly, to give a brief explanation of their respective meanings. A helpful device for sharing words with the class is to provide students a structured sentence such as, "On the topic of _____, I would like to contribute a term that I know." Students then can list the contributed words to their own Taxonomies. This activity reinforces the concept that *words are free* and are to be shared through speaking and writing.

An alternative activity for creating and sharing Taxonomies is for students to work individually and write their own words on the Taxonomy and then meet in collaborative groups to share their terms and discuss what they already know about the topic. Following the initial small-group sharing, students can contribute their words to other groups or share with the whole class. Using Taxonomy building as an advanced organizing procedure allows both the teacher and the students to have a clear sense of the collective knowledge on a specific topic.

Figure 2.2 shows the collected prior knowledge of a fourth grade class on the topic of deserts.

Continuous Notetaking

As the class studies a topic from their textbook, research materials, and/or discussion, the students use their individual Taxonomies for notetaking and for adding new terms that reflect their growing knowledge. By the end of the unit, the students have a Taxonomy that represents what they have learned or should know. The Taxonomy also can be used for review and as the basis for moving into other writing strategies.

By the completion of the unit on deserts, there might be a class Taxonomy that looks like the one shown in Figure 2.3, but students may have slightly different taxonomies resulting from individual choices.

Vocabulary Development

As the students build their Taxonomies in different subject areas, they learn and define new terms. As they first learn a word, students may simply state what a term means. If there are geographic terms, they can expand on their definitions by locating them on a map or globe. During this word-building time, the Taxonomy is being used as both the starting point for getting new knowledge and the outcome point that indicates what the students need to know about the topic. Once students become accustomed to Taxonomy building, they will have a complete vocabulary of all the topics and units they have studied in the course of a school year, plus lists of topics that personally interest them.

TAXONOMY SHEET

Deserts

A
B
C camel, cactus
D dry
E
F
G
H hot
I
J
K
L little rain
M
N
O
P
Q
R
S sand
T tents
U
V
W
X
Y
Z

Figure 2.2

Taxonomies also can be used to increase students' vocabularies beyond the usual ways of teaching words in a pre-reading lesson or by having students read more stories or books. One vocabulary-building strategy related to learning, retaining, and using high-level words is to have students learn selected words alphabetically. If a student could learn one new word a week, starting with an *A* word and ending with a *Z* word, the student obviously would know twenty-six new words. Then the cycle could start again and repeat itself—52 words, then 78 words, and so forth.

One group of innovative primary grade teachers in a low-income school used this strategy by compiling a list of words from A to Z that they felt their students were not likely to know. They called the list a "Taxonomy of Glorious Words" and used it to teach one word intensively for a week. (Intensively meant that the teachers would use the word frequently and consistently in a variety of contexts.) For example, if the targeted word was *accurate*, the teacher would remind the students to do their work *accurately*, to check their work for *accuracy*, or to always be *accurate* when they add up a column of numbers or tell an event. Furthermore, the "word of the week" was the word for the whole school, to be used in every classroom, announced by the principal over the public address system, and posted on the Taxonomy of Glorious Words poster in the entrance hallway or other visible area. Students were encouraged to use this word in their speech and their writing until it became a natural part of their language. Figure 2.4 shows the Taxonomy of Glorious Words selected by a committee of teachers.

	TAXONOMY SHEET **Deserts**
A	arid, Arabia, Africa, Asia
B	Bactrian camel, Bedouins
C	California desert, cool nights, cactus
D	dry, dromedary camel
E	Ethiopia, Egypt
F	
G	Gobi
H	hot days
I	Israel
J	
K	Kalahari
L	
M	Mojave
N	Negev, nomads
O	oasis
P	Painted Desert
Q	
R	
S	Sahara, Sinai, sparse, sandy
T	tents, treeless
U	
V	
W	watering holes, wadi
X	xeroscapes
Y	Yemen
Z	

Figure 2.3

	TAXONOMY SHEET **Glorious Words**
A	automatic, accurate, ambiguous
B	boisterous, brilliant, belligerent
C	compliment, compromise, conscientious
D	diligent, defiant, democracy
E	emulate, elegant, elated
F	frequent, flexible, famished
G	genuine, gullible, genre
H	habitat, harmony, hilarious
I	irritate, infinity, incentive
J	jovial, justice, jealousy
K	knowledge, kindle, knead
L	lenient, lament, leisure
M	miniature, metamorphosis, mature
N	narrate, nurture, negotiate
O	optimistic, optional, obstacle
P	prohibit, principle, procedure
Q	quality, quest, quaint
R	radiant, reconcile, redundant
S	sensitive, savory, superfluous
T	tangible, tentative, tender-hearted
U	unique, unanimous, united
V	visualize, verify, verbatim
W	wisdom, wilderness, wily
X	xenophobia, xeroscape, xanthous
Y	youth, yield, yearn
Z	zealous, zoology, zest

Figure 2.4

Development and Assessment of New Knowledge

As students are entering terms (or names) on their Taxonomies, they often are dealing with new information. They need to learn these terms' meanings and how they fit into the schema of the topic. This learning, of course, will occur through the usual methods of practice, study, and memory. However, since creating Taxonomies requires continuous active student participation, accompanied by cooperative involvement and discussion, followed by writing (as discussed in subsequent chapters), student learning is enhanced and more thoroughly developed.

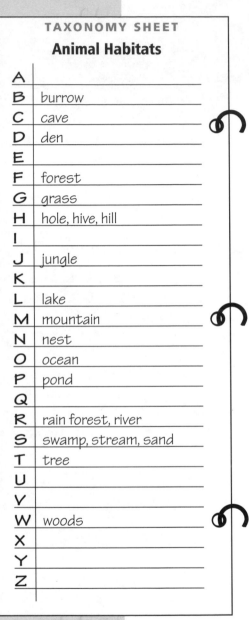

TAXONOMY SHEET
Animal Habitats

A	
B	burrow
C	cave
D	den
E	
F	forest
G	grass
H	hole, hive, hill
I	
J	jungle
K	
L	lake
M	mountain
N	nest
O	ocean
P	pond
Q	
R	rain forest, river
S	swamp, stream, sand
T	tree
U	
V	
W	woods
X	
Y	
Z	

Figure 2.5

As a lesson or topic is completed, the terms on the Taxonomy are used for evaluation and review. For example, students can create post-lesson Taxonomies by preparing a blank Taxonomy sheet and listing as many terms as possible about the topic. The quantity and relevancy of these terms are an indicator of student learning and can further serve as the basis for developing test-taking and study skills. Teachers can ask the students to put a checkmark next to those terms they feel confident they know and a question mark next to those terms they know little about. Students then can be advised to study only what they don't know or don't know well. Also, the teacher can review the Taxonomy with the students to identify what terms are significant or essential and what terms are inconsequential or trivial. Students also can use the Taxonomies to plan or create a test that they think will be a fair assessment of what they have learned. Teachers can then use or adapt this test either as a study tool or an actual evaluation.

In grades two and three, using the general topic of animals, students can develop Taxonomies such as Animal Habitats and Animal Markings and Characteristics (see Figures 2.5 and 2.6), among others. Through this categorization system, the students are involved in continuous development and assessment of new knowledge, bringing about what Hirsch points out is "active and constructive rather than passive and reconstructive" (1987, 55).

Taxonomies in the Upper Grades Through High School

While Taxonomies are valuable in all grades, they are essential in the upper grades as they become the word carriers for the topic. In the upper grades, therefore, students should maintain Taxonomies across the curriculum, from mathematics through music, and for every topic that requires in-depth factual knowledge. Following are four Taxonomies that are representative of subject area information in the middle and high schools.

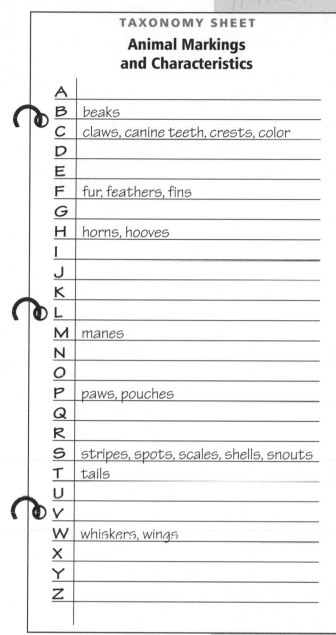

TAXONOMY SHEET

Animal Markings and Characteristics

A	
B	beaks
C	claws, canine teeth, crests, color
D	
E	
F	fur, feathers, fins
G	
H	horns, hooves
I	
J	
K	
L	
M	manes
N	
O	
P	paws, pouches
Q	
R	
S	stripes, spots, scales, shells, snouts
T	tails
U	
V	
W	whiskers, wings
X	
Y	
Z	

Figure 2.6

Directions: Write a biographic report on one of the persons below. Be sure to tell about the person's major accomplishments.

TAXONOMY SHEET

Who's Who in Flight, Astronomy, and Space?

A	Aristotle, Aldrin, Armstrong
B	Brahe, Borman, Braun (von), Bluford
C	Copernicus, Cochran, Carpenter, Chaffee
D	
E	Eratosthenes, Euclid, Earhart
F	
G	Galileo, Goddard, Gargarin, Glenn, Grissom
H	Hypatia, Halley, Herschel, Hubble
I	
J	
K	Kepler
L	Lindbergh
M	Mitchell, McAuliffe
N	Newton
O	
P	Ptolemy, Penzias
Q	
R	Ride, Resnick
S	Shapley, Schirra, Shepard, Scott
T	Tereshkova-Nicolayeva
U	
V	
W	Wright (Wilbur, Orville), Wilson, White
X	
Y	
Z	

Figure 2.7

Directions: Learn the meaning of these words and be able to illustrate them.

TAXONOMY SHEET

Terms for Polygons and Polyhedrons

A	angle
B	bilateral
C	cube, cylinder
D	decagon, dodecahedron
E	
F	
G	
H	hexagon, hexahedron, hexagram
I	
J	
K	
L	
M	
N	nonagon
O	octagon, octahedron
P	plane, pentagon, pentangle, pentahedron, polyangular, pentagram, prism, pyramid, parallelogram
Q	quadrangle, quadrilateral, quadrille
R	rectangle, rhombus
S	septagon, sphere
T	triangle, trapezoid, trihedron, tetragon, tetrahedron
U	unilateral
V	
W	
X	
Y	
Z	

Figure 2.8

Directions: Use a historic atlas to find the following locations of battles that changed the world.

TAXONOMY SHEET

Geographers' Battlefields

A	Acre, Austerlitz, Alamo
B	Borodino, Bunker Hill, Bikini Atoll
C	Chateau-Thierry
D	Dunkirk, Dien Bien Phu
E	El Alamein
F	Fort Sumter
G	Gettysburg, Gallipoli, Guadalcanal
H	Hastings
I	Iwo Jima
J	
K	
L	Little Big Horn, Lexington
M	Marathon, Marne
N	Normandy
O	
P	Port Arthur, Pearl Harbor
Q	
R	
S	Salamis, Saratoga, Somme, Stalingrad, Seoul, Saigon, Sarajevo
T	Thermopylae, Trafalger, Tannenberg
U	
V	Verdun
W	Waterloo
X	
Y	
Z	Yorktown, Ypres

Figure 2.9

Directions: How many of these words do you know? Circle the words you know and look up the meaning of the words you don't know.

TAXONOMY SHEET

Hablo Espanol

A	arroz, adobe, amigo
B	burrito
C	caballero, casa
D	dinero
E	enchilada
F	fiesta
G	gaucho, gracias, gusto
H	hacienda, hermano, hermana
I	
J	
K	
L	
M	muchacho, muchacha, maestro, mañana, mesa, mucho, momento, madre
N	niño, niña
O	
P	patio, pollo, poncho, padre, pescado
Q	
R	ranchero, redondo
S	sombrero, serape, señorita, salsa
T	taco, tortilla, tío, tía, tapas
U	
V	vaquero
W	
X	
Y	
Z	zapatos

Figure 2.10

Building Cooperative Learning Experiences

David Perkins, in his comprehensive study of schools that provide "better thinking and learning," refers to cooperative learning as one of the well-researched techniques that has provided "the know-how for successful classroom use" (1992, 228).

Creating and using Taxonomies provides an easy introduction into cooperative learning for students at all grade and ability levels. There are three aspects of Taxonomy building. First, students can work solo or with others. Solo building occurs when the individual student is developing a personal list on a topic based on her or his own prior knowledge. The second aspect occurs when students come together, bringing their individual Taxonomies to the table for sharing information. This is the collaboration or cooperative stage when the students realize that words and ideas are not only free but are valuable for expanded learning. The third aspect is the involvement of the whole class when each collaborative group shares selected items from the Taxonomies to see the whole picture, or what Hirsch calls the "unified system of background relationships" (1987, 54).

The Taxonomies in Figures 2.11, 2.12, and 2.13 illustrate a solo version, a collaborative version, and a class version all created by fourth grade students embarking on a study of animals of the woods and jungles. The teacher asked each student to set up a Taxonomy and list as many animals as possible whose natural habitat was in the woodlands or a jungle. Figure 2.11. shows a student's individually created (solo) Taxonomy based on her prior knowledge before studying this topic.

The next Taxonomy shows the Taxonomy of a collaborative group made up of several students, including the student who created the Taxonomy shown in figure 2.11.

As the class studies different animals, the students add to their Taxonomies. At the completion of the unit on woodland and jungle animals, the class Taxonomy, and each students Taxonomy, looks like the one shown in Figure 2.13. Each student now has an expanded Taxonomy for his or her Personal Thesaurus.

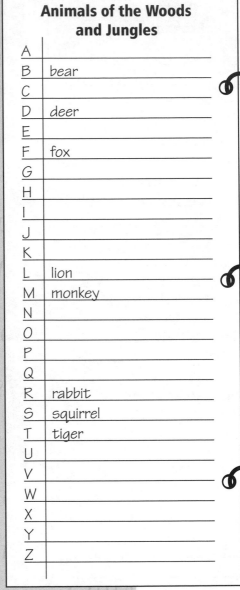

Figure 2.11

TAXONOMY SHEET	
Taxonomy of a Collaborative Group	
A	ape
B	bear, beaver
C	cheetah
D	deer
E	eagle
F	fox
G	giraffe
H	
I	
J	jaguar
K	
L	lion
M	monkey
N	
O	
P	panda
Q	
R	rabbit
S	squirrel
T	tiger
U	
V	
W	
X	
Y	
Z	zebra

Figure 2.12

TAXONOMY SHEET	
Expanded Taxonomy of a Collaborative Group	
A	antelope, ape
B	bear, beaver, baboon
C	cheetah, chimpanzee, chipmunk
D	deer
E	eagle
F	fox, field mouse
G	giraffe, gorilla
H	hyena, hippopotamus, hare
I	iguana
J	jaguar
K	
L	lion, leopard
M	monkey, mole
N	
O	otter, orangutan
P	panda, porcupine, panther, parrot
Q	
R	rabbit, raccoon
S	skunk, squirrel, snake
T	tiger
U	
V	
W	woodchuck
X	
Y	
Z	zebra

Figure 2.13

Starting to Write

Figures 2.14 and 2.15 are suggested Taxonomies that can be used early in the school year. They are based on personal knowledge in contrast to new knowledge and can easily involve all the students regardless of background or ability.

KINDERGARTEN AND FIRST GRADE

On the very first day or by the first week of school, set up a large chart with the alphabet written vertically. Head it Roster of Names. Tell the students that this list (which you later call a Taxonomy) is very important because it tells "who lives here." Over time this list will be one of the many pieces on the walls that carries the students' names. To develop the roster, ask each student to say her or his name in this way: "My name is Ebony and it begins with the letter E." Then write the student's name on the roster of names.

The teacher can then use the roster to introduce initial letter sounds, variations in spelling, alphabetical order, and information that can be graphed. By asking students questions such as the following, teachers can show students the varied information on a Taxonomy of names.

- How many students are in this class?
- Which letter has the most names?
- Which letters have no names?
- Which names sound the same but are spelled differently?
- Who can read a name that begins with the letter ___?

GRADES TWO THROUGH FIVE: BUILDING A PERSONAL IDENTITY TAXONOMY

Personal Identity Taxonomies help to prepare students for both autobiographical and biographical writing. These taxonomies should be developed as early as possible in the school year.

A Personal Identity Taxonomy contains the words that answer the question "Who am I?" By using the starting words, "I am a . . .," the students can identify themselves as a student, classmate, friend, granddaughter, and so forth. To have the students create their Taxonomies systematically for use in writing, divide this Taxonomy into categories, such as family membership, geographic membership, and personal identity.

The first category is family membership. Students can identify themselves by words that identify family relationships, such as daughter or son, sister or brother, niece or nephew, granddaughter or grandson, goddaughter or

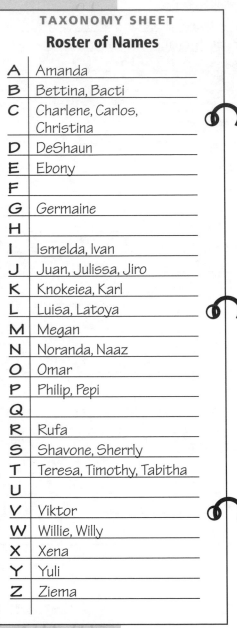

TAXONOMY SHEET
Roster of Names

A	Amanda
B	Bettina, Bacti
C	Charlene, Carlos, Christina
D	DeShaun
E	Ebony
F	
G	Germaine
H	
I	Ismelda, Ivan
J	Juan, Julissa, Jiro
K	Knokeiea, Karl
L	Luisa, Latoya
M	Megan
N	Noranda, Naaz
O	Omar
P	Philip, Pepi
Q	
R	Rufa
S	Shavone, Sherrly
T	Teresa, Timothy, Tabitha
U	
V	Viktor
W	Willie, Willy
X	Xena
Y	Yuli
Z	Ziema

Figure 2.14

godson, and cousin. Students can discuss these family membership terms and identify their own family membership terms. In addition, the teacher can model this Taxonomy for the student by creating his or her own family membership Taxonomy.

Geographic membership follows family membership. A person might be a Manhattanite, New Yorker, American, North American, and Earthling. If the student cannot form an identity term with his or her state (e.g., Connecticut), she or he can complete the statement as "I am a *Connecticut resident.*" Students discuss these geographic terms, and each student adds to her or his list. When students come from countries other than the United States, encourage them to list their first country identity as well: "I am a Dominican, a Russian, a Pakistani," and so forth. These identities can serve as topics for the strategy Where in the World (explained in a later chapter) or as part of a multicultural program or study.

Another category is personal interests and how they shape a person's identity; for example, a ball player, dancer, singer, in-line skater, reader, or movie-goer. Teachers can guide their students into thinking of themselves by using the starter "I am a . . .," and then adding their interest identity terms to their taxonomies.

Figure 2.15 shows an example of a student's Personal Identity Taxonomy, which can provide this student with ideas and topics for writing about herself.

LINKING TO THE COMPUTER

If students have frequent access to computers, the teacher can set up a blank Taxonomy format that they can copy onto their own disks or directly into their individual files. With this possibility, every student can maintain upgraded lists of terms related to subject areas as well as for personal interests. Students who know how to use graphics or desktop publishing software can decorate their taxonomies with borders and clip art. Once printed, students can put their individual taxonomies into a loose-leaf binder and truly have a published personal thesaurus.

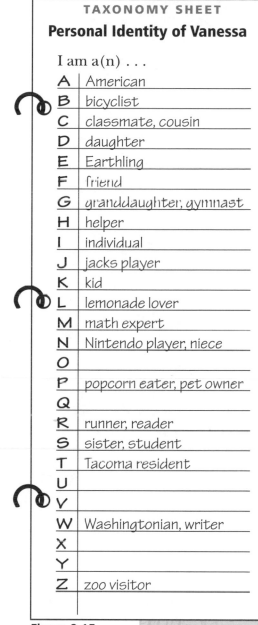

TAXONOMY SHEET
Personal Identity of Vanessa

I am a(n) . . .

A	American
B	bicyclist
C	classmate, cousin
D	daughter
E	Earthling
F	friend
G	granddaughter, gymnast
H	helper
I	individual
J	jacks player
K	kid
L	lemonade lover
M	math expert
N	Nintendo player, niece
O	
P	popcorn eater, pet owner
Q	
R	runner, reader
S	sister, student
T	Tacoma resident
U	
V	
W	Washingtonian, writer
X	
Y	
Z	zoo visitor

Figure 2.15

CHAPTER 3

Composing with Keywords

Words Define Knowledge

Every word was once a poem. Each began as a picture.

—Wilfred Funk

composing with
keywords

taxonomies

metacognition

defining format

*profiles
and frames*

who's who?

*reasons, causes,
results*

*where in
the world*

premises, premises

quotable quotes

*personifications
and interactions*

*morphology,
etymology,
and grammar*

HAVE WORDS, CAN WRITE

Every writing teacher has undoubtedly heard students moan, "I have nothing to write about" or "What do you want me to say?" These are the stomach-wrenching questions of students who feel word hungry. "Where," they wonder, "will I get the words I need to write for this assignment?" In the strategy Composing with Keywords, students use the words or terms from their Taxonomies (see chapter 2) to write sentences, paragraphs, essays, and stories.

In a study by Bereiter and Scardamalia (1985), students were asked to think of keywords they might use in an essay. Then, the students wrote an essay in which they used those words. Not surprisingly, the students had more to say and wrote more cohesively than similar-age students who were merely given a topic without this instruction. Many students have discovered the strategy of using keywords on their own, most noticeably when teachers have (unwisely) asked students to write one sentence for each spelling word. These students then (wisely) ask if they can use more than one spelling word in their sentences. What they have discovered is that they are not short-circuiting the assignment but that they are able to write more interesting and substantive sentences. Unfortunately, words on spelling lists generally are not grouped around a topic, but around some phonemic or syllabic element and are not particularly useful for writing essays or stories.

Keywords related to a specific topic can, for example, be used by students in a social studies class who have compiled a Taxonomy of major rivers of the world. The teacher might ask the students to select three or four of the rivers in Europe and write a statement about each one, telling its location, source, and mouth. In another class, the students may have compiled a Taxonomy on scary Halloween words. Here, the writing assignment might be to write a Halloween story using as many words as possible or as needed. From a Taxonomy of verbs to use for "said," students can write a story about two or three characters who never "say" anything; they only whisper, shout, laugh, murmur, bellow, or giggle.

Composing with Keywords provides students with opportunities to actually write and gain practice as writers without worrying about the more difficult aspects of topic selection and attending to the conventions of style and form. Composing with Keywords can be used often and for a variety of purposes—writing journal entries, responding to new learning, building vocabulary, and for the fun of creating unusual, unexpected, and unlikely pieces of writing. Students can share their writings in small groups, through share alouds, and on bulletin board displays, thereby gaining a concept of themselves as writers with something worth saying and worth sharing.

Creating the Unusual and the Unlikely

Teachers can introduce Composing with Keywords in the middle of first grade when students are reading stories of thirty to fifty words, and it can be continued well into the upper grades. Teachers can provide students with a blank Taxonomy sheet or have them create their own. After the students have read a story, teachers can ask them to think about which words they think tell important ideas or give useful information. For example, after reading the story *Five Little Monkeys Jumping on the Bed* by Ellen Christelow, a class of first grade students could create a Taxonomy of words from the text. After the students create their taxonomies, the teacher asks the students to select any three words and write them on a separate sheet of paper. Each student then writes a sentence using the three words. To clarify the instructions, the teacher should model her or his own sentence.

Figure 3.1 provides an example of a composite Taxonomy of words the students listed. An example of student writing using this strategy follows.

TAXONOMY SHEET

Words from
Five Little Monkeys

A	all
B	bedtime, bath
C	
D	doctor
E	
F	four, five, fall
G	go
H	
I	in
J	jumping
K	
L	
M	mama
N	never
O	one
P	pajamas
Q	
R	
S	said
T	two, three
U	
V	
W	
X	
Y	
Z	you

Figure 3.1

From this activity, the teacher compiles all of the students' writing into a class book that could be titled "Creative Sentences from the Words in *Five Little Monkeys.*"

> The **doctor** told **Mama** not to jump on the **bed.**
> One little **monkey** broke his **head** because he was **jumping** too high.
> When I was **little,** I used to **fall** out of **bed.**
> Before **bedtime** I take a **bath** and put on pajamas.

In a second grade class, the teacher guided the students in creating a Taxonomy of Tasks from which they wrote their own stories. First, the teacher asked the students to orally state what they do at home to help. A student responded, "I feed my dog." The teacher then focused on the word *feed* and wrote it on the Taxonomy. From each sentence a student said, the teacher extracted the verb. She then asked the students to think about what tasks and chores other family members do and again focused on the verbs (e.g., My mother *drives* me to school). Then the teacher gave the following instructions: Write a story about tasks or chores that you and your family do. Use as many of the words on the Taxonomy as you want to help you write the story. You can add your own words to this list. You can make your stories true or make believe.

Figure 3.2 shows a Taxonomy of Tasks that is a composite of words generated by the students.

The teacher in this class also compiled a book of the students' stories, and the students titled it "Helping at Home." Here are representative stories from the second grade students.

> First I go to the store and **buy** cat food.
> I **feed** the cat and then **clean** the litter box.
> I then help my mother **cook** dinner.
>
> I like to go **shopping** at the mall. We **drive** to the mall from my house.
> Sometimes I **buy** a Nintendo game. When I **get** home, I **sweep** the steps.
>
> I **walk** my dog and **take** out the garbage before I go to school.
> I also **wash** my Daddy's car and he **gives** me a dollar.
> Sometimes he lets me **mow** the grass.

	TAXONOMY SHEET
	Tasks
A	
B	bring, bake, buy
C	cut, cook, clean
D	drive, dust
E	
F	find, feed
G	give, get
H	hold, help
I	
J	
K	keep
L	
M	make, mix, mow
N	
O	
P	paint, plant, play
Q	
R	road, ride
S	sweep, shop
T	take
U	
V	
W	water, wash, walk
X	
Y	
Z	

Figure 3.2

Composing with Keywords for Both Factual and Fictional Writing

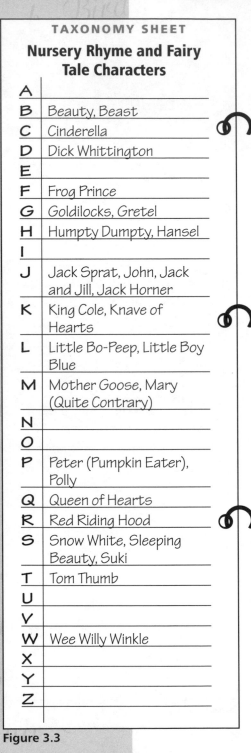

TAXONOMY SHEET

Nursery Rhyme and Fairy Tale Characters

A	
B	Beauty, Beast
C	Cinderella
D	Dick Whittington
E	
F	Frog Prince
G	Goldilocks, Gretel
H	Humpty Dumpty, Hansel
I	
J	Jack Sprat, John, Jack and Jill, Jack Horner
K	King Cole, Knave of Hearts
L	Little Bo-Peep, Little Boy Blue
M	Mother Goose, Mary (Quite Contrary)
N	
O	
P	Peter (Pumpkin Eater), Polly
Q	Queen of Hearts
R	Red Riding Hood
S	Snow White, Sleeping Beauty, Suki
T	Tom Thumb
U	
V	
W	Wee Willy Winkle
X	
Y	
Z	

Figure 3.3

In the primary grades, teachers can have students create Taxonomies of words from nursery rhymes and fairy tales. For example, one Taxonomy could contain the names of characters—Boy Blue, Bo-Peep, Goldilocks, Humpty Dumpty, and so forth. From this Taxonomy, students have the names of different characters to choose for sentence or story writing. A second Taxonomy could contain places mentioned in the rhymes or fairy tales—corner, hill, moon, hill, wall, and so forth. The third Taxonomy would be of objects and items mentioned—crown, curds and whey, fiddle, kettle, tea. Students would then be asked to select one character, one place, and one object or item and compose sentences using their three words. Figures 3.3, 3.4. and 3.5 are examples of three Taxonomies and student writing using these words.

Notice that the bolded words in the following writing sample come from each of these three Taxonomies related to the nursery rhymes.

Little Bo-Peep took her **fiddle** and climbed up the **hill**.
I asked **Humpty Dumpty** to get off the **wall** and make me some **tea**.
Little Boy Blue sat in the **corner** with a **crown** on his head.

Some teachers use this activity with their students to create ongoing projects, such as illustrating sentences, making dioramas, and creating books with titles such as *Mixed-Up Rhymes and Fairy Tales* or *Hey Diddle, Diddle, Bo-Peep, and the Fiddle*. By combining the strategies of Taxonomies and Composing with Keywords in this activity, the focus is placed on all of the following:

- Character names
- Settings
- Names of objects and items
- Innovative sentence composing
- Publication and presentation formats

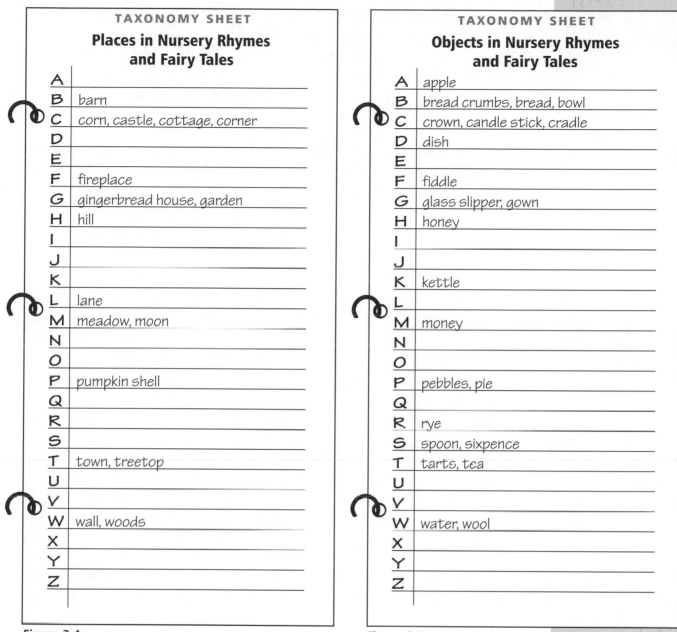

TAXONOMY SHEET

Places in Nursery Rhymes and Fairy Tales

A
B | barn
C | corn, castle, cottage, corner
D
E
F | fireplace
G | gingerbread house, garden
H | hill
I
J
K
L | lane
M | meadow, moon
N
O
P | pumpkin shell
Q
R
S
T | town, treetop
U
V
W | wall, woods
X
Y
Z

Figure 3.4

TAXONOMY SHEET

Objects in Nursery Rhymes and Fairy Tales

A | apple
B | bread crumbs, bread, bowl
C | crown, candle stick, cradle
D | dish
E
F | fiddle
G | glass slipper, gown
H | honey
I
J
K | kettle
L
M | money
N
O
P | pebbles, pie
Q
R | rye
S | spoon, sixpence
T | tarts, tea
U
V
W | water, wool
X
Y
Z

Figure 3.5

Responding to New Learning

Students in the middle grades can keep reading logs as they read a book or literature selection. In these logs, they can create Taxonomies of characters and keywords. Each day, they write what they remembered about the story using the words from the Taxonomy, adding details to each successive entry. Following are sample entries from a sixth grader's reading log of *Robin Hood*.

First piece of writing

Robin Hood was an **outlaw** who lived with his **Merry Men** in Sherwood Forest. Some of his Merry Men were **Alan-a-Dale, Will Scarlet,** and **Little John. Maid Marian** was his girlfriend. All of Robin Hood's men were good with a bow and arrow, but Robin Hood was the best **archer** of all.

Second piece of writing

When Robin Hood was nineteen years old, the king's **forester** challenged him to an **archery match** to see who could shoot a deer from a hundred yards. Robin Hood won and made the forester very angry. When Robin Hood refused to leave the forest, the forester shot an arrow at him. Robin shot back and killed the forester. From that time on, the **King John** declared that Robin Hood was an **outlaw** and told **the Sheriff of Nottingham** to find and hang Robin Hood. The king said that killing anyone who worked for him was an act of **treason** and **punishment** was death. But Robin Hood and his men were **clever** and **tricky** and always fooled the Sheriff and King John.

A list of words related to a specific topic represent the key ideas of that topic and can be used to generate ideas for an actual piece of writing. Throughout the grades, students continuously learn new subject matter terms, yet they rarely compose with these terms. Students should be given opportunities to create both factual and fictional writing using content-specific vocabulary. Students can use their Taxonomies of Mathematical Terms to create factual writing that reinforces their mathematical knowledge and fictional writing that allows them to apply this knowledge in creative and whimsical ways. When studying verbs, students can compile taxonomies of different types of verbs and then compose the "real" or "unreal" pieces of writing. Each topical- or subject-area Taxonomy can provide the springboard for a wide range of writing.

Here are five examples that represent student writing developed from Taxonomies in different subject areas.

From a Taxonomy on Numbers

Fractions are special kinds of **numbers.** They have a **numerator** and **denominator** and are not **whole numbers.** They are also different from **integers** because an integer can only be **one, two, three,** and so forth. Sometimes a fraction is actually a **mixed number** when the numerator is larger than the denominator. If you want to add fractions, you must be sure that they have **common denominators.** To do this, you need to find the **factors** for each fraction you are adding.

Fifth grade student

SkyLight Professional Development

From a Taxonomy on Verbs of Movement
Each animal has its own way of moving. A horse can **trot, canter,** or **gallop.**
A cat might **run, scoot,** or **climb.** Birds **hop, fly, glide,** and **soar.** Elephants
usually **lumber,** but when they are trained to be in the circus, they **dance,**
prance, and **twirl.** Monkeys **lope** and **swing,** ducks **waddle** and **swim,** and
jaguars **speed** and **pounce.** Humans can **move** in almost as many ways as
the animals, but they are not always as fast or as graceful as the animals.

Seventh grade student

From a Taxonomy Related to Understanding and Accepting Differences
Even though people may look and act differently, they also are alike in many
ways. They may have different **religions,** speak different **languages,** and
have different **skin color,** but they do many of the same things. They live in
family groups, love their children, and have **spiritual beliefs.** By looking at
how we are the same instead of how we are different, we learn to **accept**
and **respect** each other.

Eighth Grade Student

From a Taxonomy on Land Forms
Take a trip in a small, low-flying airplane and you will see a **landscape** of
forms and shapes that are either below sea level or soar high into the
atmosphere. If you are flying over New Mexico, you will see the flat-topped
mesas above the dry **arroyos** and the stretches of **desert.** Then head
north to Colorado to glimpse the **Grand Canyon** and continue towards the
Rockies. Take out your binoculars and peer into sharp-cut **gorges** and
deep **valleys** surrounded by snow-capped **peaks.** Beneath the snow line of
the **mountains** are evergreen **forests** looking down upon the **river banks**
that are waiting for the river to flood and quench their parched **soil.**

Tenth grade student

From a Taxonomy of Mathematical Terms Employed in a
Language Arts Class
I had to **borrow** my brother's car so that I could **join** my friend Martha who
lived about **twenty kilometers** from my house. I **owed** Martha a visit
because she had come to see me a **number** of **times** when I was sick. I felt
that since Martha had always given me her **undivided** attention, I needed
to give her **equal time.** I wanted to be at Martha's house by **one o'clock** so
that we could have lunch and **exchange** stories. Unfortunately my brother
had forgotten to **add** water to the car engine and the **temperature** on the
heating gauge was climbing rapidly. So on the way to Martha's house, I had
to stop at a **Seven-Eleven** gas station and wait for the heating gauge to
register **zero** before I could put in a cooling liquid. Then my troubles **multi-**
plied. I was supposed to make a **right angle** turn where **Division** Street

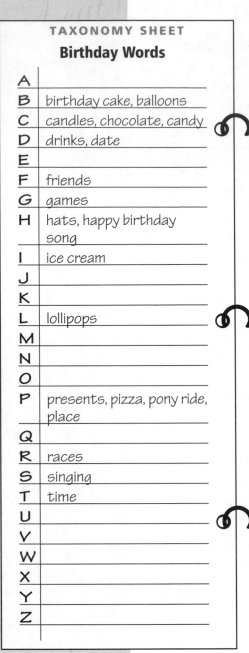

TAXONOMY SHEET
Birthday Words

A	
B	birthday cake, balloons
C	candles, chocolate, candy
D	drinks, date
E	
F	friends
G	games
H	hats, happy birthday song
I	ice cream
J	
K	
L	lollipops
M	
N	
O	
P	presents, pizza, pony ride, place
Q	
R	races
S	singing
T	time
U	
V	
W	
X	
Y	
Z	

Figure 3.6

intersected with **Fourth** Ave, but instead I turned left. After traveling for **six** blocks, I found myself **perpendicular** to a fence on a dead end street. If I didn't turn around quickly, I would be going in **circles**. Luckily, I got back to the **intersection** I needed and turned left which, of course, was now right. I **calculated** that a **fifteen minute** trip had taken me an **hour,** but Martha was not a person who **measured** lateness. She had a **rational** mind about delays and **problems** and **totally** welcomed me into her house.

A high school student

Keywords for Journal Entries

Teachers often are concerned that journal writing may become repetitive and/or trivial. Unless prompted or given ideas or topics, students frequently find themselves at a loss for keeping their journal entries varied and lively. When teachers provide or suggest keywords either from Taxonomies or text materials, students come up with new ideas for their journals. Following are examples of journal entries based on Composing with Keywords that could have been written by students from two different grade levels.

Early Primary Example: Birthday Taxonomy

Teacher prompt: For your journal entry, imagine that you are planning a birthday party. First, create a Taxonomy of Birthday Words. Then, make an exciting invitation to the party. Use as many words from your Taxonomy as you can.

The students then "plan" an invitation in their journals, writing different parts of the journal on different pages. Figure 3.7 shows an example written by a third grade student.

Middle School Example: Nutritional Words

In a middle school language arts class, students can create a Taxonomy of Nutritional Foods. The teacher first asks the students to keep track of the foods they were eating over a week's time and record this information in their journals. After a week's time, the students are asked to write a detailed statement telling which foods they liked the most, how these foods had been prepared, and whether they would continue eating them. Students should include as many words as possible from their Taxonomy of Nutritional Foods. Following is a statement that could result from such

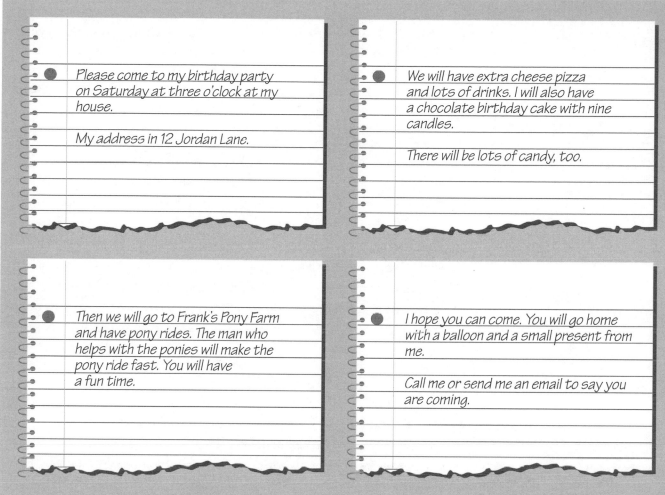

Figure 3.7 Third Grade Student Sample

Please come to my birthday party on Saturday at three o'clock at my house.

My address in 12 Jordan Lane.

We will have extra cheese pizza and lots of drinks. I will also have a chocolate birthday cake with nine candles.

There will be lots of candy, too.

Then we will go to Frank's Pony Farm and have pony rides. The man who helps with the ponies will make the pony ride fast. You will have a fun time.

I hope you can come. You will go home with a balloon and a small present from me.

Call me or send me an email to say you are coming.

an assignment. (The words that appear in bold are from the Taxonomy of Nutritional Foods.)

When I began this project on nutritional foods, I hated **broccoli, cabbage,** and **red peppers.** I didn't care how much **vitamin C** they had. I had never heard the word **antioxidants** and I really didn't care. I wanted my **chicken** to be fried and I wasn't going to worry about **cholesterol.** But then my mother found some good **low fat** recipes and good ways to cook these foods I hated. She made the broccoli with a little bit of **olive oil** and **garlic.** She put a little bit of cabbage and red peppers on some **lettuce** and then made a dressing with the taste of **peanuts.** I've now changed my mind about eating broccoli, cabbage, and red peppers.

Keywords for Vocabulary Building

At any grade level, students can compose stories with new vocabulary from readers, literature, or content areas. Following are two writing examples, one by a sixth grade student who was studying weather in a science class and the other by a high school student who had to read *The Pearl* by John Steinbeck. (Bolded words are from the students' texts.)

Weather Vocabulary

In the summer in New York City, everyone complains about the **humidity,** which is the amount of water in the air. On a hot day, when there is moisture in the air, we feel even hotter than when it is dry. **Meteorologists** know exactly how much humidity there is by using an instrument called a **hygrometer,** which uses hair that stretches when it's wet and shrinks when it's dry. Then, in winter, everyone complains because of high winds, cold weather fronts, and ice crystals on the trees. Now the meteorologists are using instruments like **anemometers** to measure wind speed, **barometers** to measure air pressure, and **satellites** to track air movements and storms.

Vocabulary from The Pearl

The story The Pearl is considered a **parable,** a story that teaches a moral lesson. The lesson is about the **avarice** or greed of a rich doctor who refuses to help cure a poor couple's baby because they haven't the money to pay him. The couple is too proud to beg for **alms**—food or money. They do not want to be considered **supplicants**—beggars without a trade. Yet the couple is terrified that their baby, who has been bitten by a scorpion, will die without medicine. They stand outside the church and pray that the priest will offer a **benediction,** a blessing, on their child even though they are poor.

LINKING TO THE COMPUTER

Composing with Keywords is an excellent strategy for helping students write independently using the computer. Teachers can have students select a Taxonomy either of their choice or one that relates to a current topic. Then, they can select anywhere from three to five words and write or copy them onto a document called Keyword Composing (or any other appropriate title).

Following are several suggestions for student writing activities using a computer.

Students . . .

- write one sentence using the words found on Taxonomies they've constructed. The sentence should tell something about the topic.

- write one sentence using the words found on Taxonomies they've constructed. The sentence should not be about the topic, but could be something imaginative or make believe.

- write a paragraph using the words selected from the Taxonomies they've constructed. The paragraph should have a topic sentence and three or four detailed sentences. The student may need to go back to his or her Taxonomy and select additional words.

- select three to five words from three different Taxonomies. They write a story using as many of the words as possible.

$\mathcal{M}$etacognition

Knowing What You Know

Once . . . relevant knowledge has been acquired, the skill follows.

—E. D. Hirsch Jr.

WHAT IS METACOGNITION?

Metacognition refers to the conscious awareness of what one knows or doesn't know. It includes both what a person knows deeply and what a person knows on the surface. It also includes what one needs to know in order to achieve his or her goals or objectives. Arthur Costa (1991) includes metacognition as one of the essential characteristics of intelligent human behavior that, together with curiosity and wonderment, motivate people to seek additional knowledge. The concept of metacognition is elaborated upon by David Perkins, who defines four levels of metacognitive learners: tacit learners who are unaware of their knowledge, aware learners who know about some of the kinds of thinking they do, strategic learners who are problem solvers and decision makers, and, finally, reflective learners who "ponder their strategies and revise them" (Perkins 1992, 102). Teachers generally find that successful or achieving students are aware of what they already know about a particular topic (prior knowledge); they recognize what they have learned that they didn't know before (new knowledge), and they identify what they need to know to meet requirements or standards (expected knowledge).

Many teachers use the concepts underlying metacognition when they teach KWL, a procedure developed by Donna Ogle (1986) that asks the student to identify for themselves "what I know," "what I want to know," and "what I have learned." Through this procedure, the learner can

taxonomies

composing with keywords

metacognition

defining format

profiles and frames

who's who?

reasons, causes, results

where in the world

premises, premises

quotable quotes

personifications and interactions

morphology, etymology, and grammar

conceptualize or visualize what she or he already understands and then keep track of new understandings that accrue.

METACOGNITION THROUGH WRITING

In this strategy, the students begin by writing what they believe they already know about a specific topic. The purpose of this writing is to develop an awareness of prior knowledge in preparation for adding new knowledge. Metacognition requires reflection on what one has already learned and what one either needs to know or would like to know. When used extensively in every subject and throughout the grades, metacognition (through writing) fosters curiosity to learn more (Costa 1991) and provides strategies for knowing how to learn more (Perkins 1992). Students who use this strategy before, during, and after learning a new topic develop a skill for acquiring and applying knowledge, thereby making the move from tacit learners to reflective learners. Following is a plan for metacognition through writing.

Before starting a new topic, teachers can ask students to write what they believe they already know about that topic, using the sentence starter "I know that I know something about. . . ."

The students complete the statement (e.g., "I know that I know something about the Mississippi River") and then write one, two, or three sentences (depending on grade level and/or ability) that tell what they know. At the conclusion of the writing, the students add, "Now you know something that I know about. . . ."

Here is the prior knowledge statement of a fifth grade student writing in a social studies class.

Metacognition—Prior Knowledge

> I know that I know something about the Mississippi River. It is a very long river in the United States. It is in the state of Mississippi. Many steamboats travel on this river. Now you know something that I know about the Mississippi River.

The student then studies the Mississippi River through readings and class discussions, completes a Taxonomy, and Composes with Keywords. The student then writes a Metacognitive Statement to indicate new knowledge, as shown in the following example.

Metacognition—New Knowledge

> After reading my social studies book and looking at a map of the United States, I now know more about the Mississippi River than I knew before. I now know that the Mississippi begins in the northern part of the United States at Lake Superior. It touches the states of Minnesota, Wisconsin, Michigan, Iowa, Illinois, Missouri, Kentucky, Tennessee, Arkansas, Mississippi, and Louisiana. It meets the Ohio River in southern Illinois and empties into the Gulf of Mexico in New Orleans. This is some of the important information I know about the Mississippi River.

For the final piece of writing, the student adds his or her recognition of the following knowledge.

Metacognition—Advanced Knowledge

> I further know that other rivers besides the Ohio flow into the Mississippi. They are the Missouri, the Red, and the Arkansas Rivers. The Mississippi River is 3,779 kilometers or 2,348 miles long. Many cities are on the river. Some of these cities are St. Paul, Dubuque, Hannibal, St. Louis, Memphis, Vicksburg, Baton Rouge, and New Orleans. Many boats travel on the river today, not only steamboats. Sometimes this river has terrible floods that destroy homes and farms. The last flood was in 1993 and I hope there will be no more for a long time. This is my advanced knowledge about the Mississippi River. I now know much more about the Mississippi River than anyone else in my family.

Starting Sentences for Metacognitive Writing

One of the easiest ways to start a metacognitive piece of writing is to use starting sentences. The complexity of the information to be elicited can vary based on the students' level of expertise and knowledge. Starting sentences offer many students—especially beginning writers and writers who have trouble thinking of what to write—a way to get started. Teachers can provide students a list of sample starting sentences or brainstorm starting sentences with students. Lists can be posted in the classroom or copied into students' writing notebooks for reference. Following are several sample starting sentences.

Starting Sentences

- ▪ Before I read _____, I only knew these facts (or this information).

- As I listened (read, watched) _____, I better understood (realized, learned) _____.
- After I heard _____, I remembered (thought about, considered) _____.
- As a result of reading (hearing, listening to, studying, observing)_____, I now can _____.

Starters also can be variations of "I know."

- I know that I know a lot about . . .
- I know that I know something about . . .
- I know many things about . . .
- I need to know more about . . .
- I know very little about . . .
- I know nothing about . . .
- I would like to know more about . . .

A fourth grade student used one of the starters to write the following Metacognition paragraph.

> I know that I know something about rivers. Rivers flow but I don't know what makes them flow. I know something about the Hudson River, but I don't anything about other rivers. The Hudson River has a lot of bridges across it. One is called the Tappan Zee Bridge. That is what I know about rivers so far.

Using Taxonomies to Write Metacognitive Statements

As soon as students are able to write, they can compose Metacognitive statements based on the many things they already know about and the new information they are learning. For primary students and students who benefit from visual prompts, teachers can develop a Taxonomy with the students using the sentence "I know that I know something about . . ." and post it in the classroom or have students put it in their Personal Thesaurus notebooks. From these topics, students can write about what they know in their journals or can share information with classmates during a class activity. The topics on the Taxonomy also can be related to materials from readers and other texts, followed by the students writing metacognitive statements on these topics. For example, if the students will be reading about kittens, they first can write what they already know, and then write about "I now know. . . ." Figure 4.1 shows a sample Taxonomy for young students.

Using the "I know that I know something about" Taxonomy, primary students wrote the following metacognitive writings.

> I know about my Mommy. She is good to me. She reads to me. She makes me take a bath. Now you know about my Mommy.
>
> *Kindergarten student*

> I know that I know something about ice cream. It can be chocolate or vanilla. If you're a grown up it can be something like pistachino (sic) which is green. It comes in a cone or a cup or sometimes on a stick. Now you know something about ice cream.
>
> *First grade student*

> My teacher read us Charlotte's Web and now I know what a runt is. It's a baby pig that is too small to live. So sometimes the farmer wants to kill it before it dies by itself. Wilbur was a runt, but Fern saved him from dying. Now I know what a runt pig is.
>
> *Third grade student*

Using Metacognitive Writing to Consolidate Writing with Subject Areas

By the middle grades, students can reinforce their learning by writing metacognitive statements on a daily basis and for a variety of subject areas. The teacher can post a chart or agenda for the day that shows topics students can write about to sum up what they know, have learned, or need to learn. Assignments may look something like this:

- Mathematics: After you have finished adding fractions with mixed denominators, write a metacognitive statement telling what you now know about fractions.

- Social studies: We will be starting a unit on the Constitution. Write a metacognitive statement telling three ideas that you believe are in the Constitution.

- Science: After you have read the section on "How Plants Make Their Food," write a metacognitive statement telling three new ideas that you learned as a result of your reading.

TAXONOMY SHEET
I Know That I Know Something About . . .

A	animals
B	babies
C	carrots
D	Daddies
E	eggs
F	friends
G	grandmas and grandpas
H	houses
I	ice cream
J	jump rope
K	kittens
L	lemonade
M	mommies
N	nighttime
O	owls
P	paper
Q	quilts
R	running
S	school
T	television
U	umbrellas
V	voices
W	water
X	x rays
Y	yellow
Z	zoos

Figure 4.1

■ Literature: Now that you have read the story of "Arachne and Athena," write a metacognitive statement with this opening "Before I read this story I did not know (or understand). . . . However, I now know (or understand). . . .

Using Pre- and Post-Metacognition Writing

Students at the middle school or high school level often remember more and have better understanding of topics when they write pre-metacognition statements, later followed by post-metacognitive statements. While similar to the previously mentioned prior knowledge statements, these differ in that students write *two* metacognitive statements, which allows them to *compare* what they knew before the lesson(s) and after the lesson(s). These pre- and post-statements are excellent for students to use in small cooperative groups of three or four where they can discuss what they first thought about the topic and what they have since learned. Better yet is when students in these groups add information they have heard from their classmates to their own writing. This system of pre- and post-writing is far more effective for selecting and reporting knowledge than answering questions from the back of the chapter and then *copying* the text to satisfy the question. Following are examples of teacher prompts and student responses using metacognition.

American history

Teacher Prompt: Today we will be discussing the Reconstruction Period after the Civil War. Using the Metacognition format, write what you think happened in America during this period of time.

Student's response before teacher's presentation
I know that after the Civil War the former slaves could not find jobs. They had no skills except what they did as slaves which was picking cotton or working in the master's house. The government would have to find a way to help both the slaves and the soldiers who had fought in the war. I think this is why this time was called Reconstruction.

Student's response after teacher's presentation
In today's class discussion, I learned that the southern governments that were in the Civil War passed laws that were called Black Codes. These laws made blacks pay high taxes if they worked at jobs that were not on a farm or plantation. These taxes made blacks go back to where they lived before the war and do the same kind of work. There were many other laws against blacks. They could not buy land or own guns or even dogs. The worse thing was that their children could be taken from them if their old masters said

they were unfit parents. Then the children would practically be slaves again to the masters who had taken them away from their family. I now realize that even though slavery was supposed to end because the North won the Civil War, blacks were not yet free or better off.

Eleventh grade student

Combining Strategies: Metacognitve Statement and Composing with Keywords

With the Taxonomy as the "holder" of the terms or vocabulary of a topic, the students have *words* for writing. Now they must select or draw upon those words that they find meaningful or significant to the topic. The students are becoming cognitive decision makers, making decisions as to what they will write about. Thus, with the words they have selected from the Taxonomy and with the opening metacognitive statement, students have what to say and a format for saying it. This arrangement is especially comfortable for students who ordinarily find writing difficult.

The following example is from a literature class studying Paul Zindel's novel *The Pigman*. Here the students used the strategy Composing with Keywords (see chapter 3) to write metacognitive statements that expressed their insights on loneliness as it related to the central character in the story, Mr. Pignati. The students first created a Taxonomy of words that describe loneliness (see Figure 4.2).

Next, the students selected three terms from the Taxonomy and wrote what they knew or understood about Mr. Pignati's loneliness. Following is an example written by an eighth grade student.

> The three words of loneliness that help me better understand Mr. Pignati are alienated, ostracized, and unfulfilled. To be alienated means to be unattached to the world, something like an alien. That is how Mr. Pignati feels after his wife dies. He seems to have very little understanding of what people outside of his world do or feel is correct. Because he can't relate to other people and they can't relate to him, he is ostracized, meaning that no one, except Lorraine and John, want to associate with him. Finally I know that he is unfulfilled in his hopes and dreams. No one

TAXONOMY SHEET	
Alone, Alone, All Alone: The Sad Vocabulary of Loneliness	
A	alone, alienated, abandoned, avoided
B	bored, bereft
C	
D	depressed, detached, disconnected, desolate
E	
F	friendless, forsaken
G	
H	homesick, helpless
I	ignored
J	jilted
K	
L	lonely
M	melancholy
N	
O	ostracized
P	
Q	
R	removed, rejected
S	sad, solemn, solitary, shut-in, shunned
T	tired
U	unfulfilled
V	
W	weary
X	
Y	
Z	xenophobic

Figure 4.2

appreciates his collection of pigs or can even understand what this collection means to him. I feel sad for Mr. Pignati because I know and feel what loneliness does to destroy a person's sense of worth.

LINKING TO THE COMPUTER

Metacognitive writing lends itself to using a template that provides a structure for student writers. The template can consist of sentence starters that prompt the writer to reflect on what he or she knows, wants to know, or knows following learning about a specific topic. The teacher can create a template in a word processing program, save it on disk or the computer's hard drive, and make it available to students when they use computers for writing. Charts showing the template can be posted above the computers for easy reference. Following are examples that can be used at different grade levels.

Primary

Metacognition—What Do I Know That I Know?

I know that I know something about

First, I know _____

I also know _____

Finally, I know _____

Now you know something that I know about _____

Metacognition—What Would I Like to Know?

I would like to know more about _____

First, I would like to know why _____

Then I would like to know where _____

Last, I would like to know when _____

These are some of the things I would like to know about_____

Metacognition—What Do I Need to Know?

I need to know how to _____

Then I would be able to _____

I would also be able to _____

Finally, I could _____

These are the reasons I need to know how to _____

Middle School and Secondary Grades

Metacognition—I Know What I Know

In my (subject area) class, I know that I know or understand several important ideas.

First, I know/understand _____

In addition, I _____

Furthermore, I _____

I am now prepared to _____

Metacognition—As a Result of . . . I Now . . .

As a result of (reading, studying, listening, discussing), I now (realize, recognize, think about, dream of) _____

I better understand _____

Furthermore, I believe _____

Above all, I _____

This new (knowledge, discovery, idea, thought) will help me _____

_____

Metacognition—Present Knowledge to Future Knowledge

In my class, I have been studying (learning)

When I began this topic, I knew

    1) _____

    2) _____

    3) _____

Over the next few weeks (months), I expect to know

    1) _____

    2) _____

    3) _____

This new knowledge will _____

As students develop the habit of writing metacognitive statements, they gain a greater sense of ownership of their learning. They have a tangible representation of how much knowledge they started with and how much knowledge they are adding and can add. Metacognitive writing can be compared to setting up one of those charts or "thermometers" that are used to record fund-raising results: "Here is where I began, here is how much I have achieved to date, and here is where I have to go."

CHAPTER 5

Defining Format

Categorizing and Clarifying

> . . . *it is in word meaning that thought and speech unite in verbal thought.*
>
> —Lev Vygotsky

DEFINING FORMAT—CONSTRUCTING MEANING

Every day students are likely to hear their teachers ask a question framed as "What is (a) . . .?" as in "What is a river?" "What is a mammal?" "What is a triangle?" and so forth. Then the students struggle to explain the term, giving answers such as "A river is water like a lake but different," "A mammal is an animal with fur," or "A triangle is something with three sides." When the students are asked to further elaborate on the definition, they are likely to add more "pieces" in haphazard order: "Well, a river is long, not round like a lake," "A mammal also has live babies," "A triangle has three angles."

The problem with these partial responses is just that—they are partial. Students who are uninstructed in defining terms may fail to categorize an item (e.g., "A river is a body of water"), leave out essential information, or resort to using the word *something* as a bridge to explaining the term. When students try to define common terms, they often have great difficulty. A pencil is "something to write with," rain is "when water falls from the sky," and a flag is "what waves."

The defining problem gets even worse when students look up a term in the dictionary and are confronted with information that either is too sparse or too diverse and then merely copy the words. The ability to clearly define terms is essential to understanding them. Students must be taught *how* to define so they won't get tangled in a maze of words that leaves both the definer and the audience confused. The instructional strategy Defining Format aids students in defining terms and can be used whenever students must formulate well-defined explanations of what they know or need to know. The format has three parts: asking the question, stating the category, and listing the characteristics. The student asks a question (e.g., What is a river?). Then the student turns the question into a statement that begins " A _____ is a _____ " (e.g.,"A river is a"). The article "a" (or "an") is essential to state the category (e.g., A river is a body of water"). Following the category, the student numerically lists the characteristics of the term being defined. Students can use a visual organizer, such as the one shown in figure 5.1, as a tool to work through each part of the format.

DEFINING FORMAT
What is a River?

Question	Category	Characteristics
What is a river? A river is a	body of water that	1. flows into another body of water such as a lake, a bay, a gulf, or the ocean 2. has a source and a mouth 3. forms banks on each side 4. begins with fresh water that may become brackish and then salty 5. may flow north or south 6. may have rapids or meander

Figure 5.1

The visual organizer is made up of three columns, two that are narrow and one that is wide. The purpose of this setup is to help the writer categorize the item and then list the characteristics that make the item different from other items in the *same category*. Once a student has defined one term in a category, he or she can define other terms in the same category. For example, the student who defines a river could subsequently define a *lake* or *bay* or *ocean* by stating that these too are *bodies of water* but with different characteristic or qualities. When two or more terms in the same category are defined using the Defining Format strategy, the student can use the defining information to compare the items, as shown in the following example that compares a river and a lake.

We can compare a river with a lake in several ways. Both are bodies of water, but with different characteristics. A river begins at a source that is usually in high land and flows north or south towards its mouth. The mouth is where it empties into another body of water such as a lake, a bay, or the ocean. A lake is a body of water that is surrounded on all sides by land and may get its water from a river flowing into it. Rivers are thought of as long and lakes are thought of as large. Both rivers and lakes can have fresh water, brackish water, or salt water.

Sixth grade student

USING DEFINING FORMAT

In the Primary Grades

Defining Format can be introduced as early as the first grade and continued throughout the grades. Young students easily understand its use because it begins with the kind of question they have asked since their preschool days: "What is [that]?" The response is simply a reframing: "[That] is a. . . . " The teaching aspect of this strategy is guiding or directing the students toward stating the category rather than using the word *something;* for example, What is a jacket? A jacket is a type of clothing (not *something* you wear). By helping students to state the category, the teacher shows them how items can be classified or categorized. In many cases, teachers can move from the Defining Format into creating a Taxonomy of words related to the category (e.g., types of clothing).

Teachers can begin by setting up the Defining Format visual organizer on a large sheet of chart paper and telling the students that they will be helping to explain the meaning of words they already know to a Martian—someone who is not likely to know what the items are. In writing to a Martian, a person must be very clear and precise. A good starting word for young students to define is the word *dog* since most young people know what a dog is but have not yet thought much about the essential characteristics that make a dog a dog (and not a fox or wolf). Students likely will define a dog as "an animal that barks," which can be used as a starting phrase to further define *dog* using the Defining Format strategy. The teacher can probe for more information. By completing the visual organizer, the teacher can show students how to write a definition using this strategy. Figure 5.2 shows a completed format from a first grade class.

DEFINING FORMAT		
What is a Dog?		
Question	Category	Characteristics
What is a dog? A dog is an	animal that	1. barks 2. has four legs and a tail 3. has fur or hair 4. has puppies 5. is a pet 6. can learn to sit or get a ball 7. knows its name 8. walks on a leash 9. takes care of you and licks you 10. has many breeds

Figure 5.2

As students learn more about the topic or item, they add to the format. When the students have completed their Defining Formats, they can write a metacognitive statement using the information they have gathered. Using the dog example, the starting sentence for the metacognitive statement could be "I know many facts about a dog" or "I know five important facts about a dog."

After introducing the Defining Format, the teacher can set up a Taxonomy of terms that students can define, similar to the one shown in figure 5.3.

Because many primary students may know the basic characteristics of the items but do not know how to categorize them, the teacher may provide the categories until the students have learned them. Following are several ways this can be done.

- Simply tell the students; for example, "Rain is called *precipitation*. Snow, hail, and sleet also belong to the category of precipitation."

- Offer the starter; for example, "A tree is a type of. . . ."

- Set up a Taxonomy of categories to which students can refer. For example, the Taxonomy shown in Figure 5.4 gives categories for the terms shown in Figure 5.3.

In many cases, the teacher will need to express the category with the phrase *type of* as in type of fruit or type of vehicle. With frequent use of the Defining Format, students become more skilled in defining a term by stating its category and listing its characteristics.

TAXONOMY SHEET
Terms We Have Defined

A	apple
B	bicycle
C	carrot
D	dog
E	
F	farm
G	
H	Halloween
I	ice cream
J	
K	king
L	
M	monkey
N	
O	
P	pet
Q	
R	rain
S	
T	tree
U	
V	violin
W	
X	xylophone
Y	
Z	zoo

Figure 5.3

TAXONOMY SHEET
Categories

A	animal
B	building
C	clothing
D	dessert, dwelling
E	emotion
F	fruit
G	game
H	holiday
I	
J	
K	
L	
M	musical instrument, mammal
N	
O	
P	plant, precipitation, place
Q	
R	
S	subject
T	timepiece
U	
V	vehicle, vegetable
W	
X	
Y	
Z	

Figure 5.4

Using Defining Format for More Complex Terms

As students move into the intermediate grades and middle school, they are inundated with content area terminology, especially in social studies and science. Words such as *colony, state, country, pioneer, revolution* become part of the expected vocabulary terrain of middle grade students. A few students will grasp the full meanings of these words. Unfortunately, others will have only a vague or superficial understanding of where one term ends and another begins. Many students often remain fuzzy about even commonly used words. When students in a sixth grade class were asked to define the word *planet,* some students responded by saying, "It's a big round ball in the sky" and "It's something [that word again!] that goes around the sun." Of greater significance, many students, when given a list of words to *define,* assume that *define* means copy. Using a glossary or a dictionary, they merely transfer to their notebooks what they have trouble understanding in the first place. One student in a social studies class, when asked to define referendum, copied the meaning verbatim from the textbook's glossary and when asked to explain the meaning in her own words, was startled by the question. Her answer was, "It's what it says it is in the glossary."

By high school, students should be accustomed to setting up their definitions of content area terms using the Defining Format. Hopefully, they will think in terms of categories rather than discrete items, so that for each content area, they define terms based on the categories specific to that content area. For mathematics, students would define a number as a symbol, addition as an operation, a trapezoid as a polygon, and so forth. In geography and earth science, students would think in terms of landforms or bodies of water; in health, they would classify terms by body systems or chemical substances. The literature teacher points out the literary genres, and the art teacher has the students group and define by art form genres.

Figure 5.5, 5.6, 5.7, 5.8, 5.9, and 5.10 are examples of several Defining Formats for terms students frequently encounter in their studies but rarely define with clarity.

Social Studies Examples

DEFINING FORMAT		
What is a Colony?		
Question	Category	Characteristics
What is a colony? A colony is a	type of community that	1. is composed of people who have chosen to live together for a common purpose or goal 2. may have its own local form of government but is generally governed by a larger or more powerful government 3. may be composed of one or several settlements 4. was formed in the early years after the discovery of the American continents
		Add Other Appropriate Information

Figure 5.5

DEFINING FORMAT
What is a Slave?

Question	Category	Characteristics
What is a slave? A slave is a	person who*	1. is owned by another person and is considered to be property 2. is unable to own his or her possessions 3. works without wages, but is provided with food, clothing, and shelter according to the owner's wishes 4. does not have rights as a parent to raise or keep one's children 5. can be bought and sold at the owner's desire
	*Notice the use *who* when defining a person	Add Other Appropriate Information

Figure 5.6

Science Examples

DEFINING FORMAT
What is a Planet?

Question	Category	Characteristics
What is a planet? A planet is a	body in space (or heavenly body) that	1. orbits around the sun 2. is made of gases and other related matters 3. may rotate on its axis 4. may have moons or rings <div align="right">Add Other Appropriate Information</div>

Figure 5.7

DEFINING FORMAT
What is a Cell?

Question	Category	Characteristics
What is a cell? A cell is a	structural unit that	1. is the basis of all plant and animal life 2. may be a complete organism or a part of other organisms 3. has a surrounding membrane and a substance called cytoplasm 4. contains the genetic material known as DNA 5. is composed of oxygen, hydrogen, carbon, and nitrogen <div align="right">Add Other Appropriate Information</div>

Figure 5.8

Mathematics Examples

DEFINING FORMAT		
What is Addition?		
Question	Category	Characteristics
What is addition? Addition is a	mathematical operation that	1. requires two or more numbers, called addends, to get a sum 2. may be written horizontally (2 + 6 = 8) or vertically $\quad 2$ $\qquad +\underline{6}$ $\qquad 8$ 3. when written vertically is written with one number under the other by place value 4. may use a plus sign, an equal sign, or an underline bar 5. is the basis of multiplication
		Add Other Appropriate Information

Figure 5.9

DEFINING FORMAT		
What is a Triangle?		
Question	Category	Characteristics
What is a triangle? A triangle is a	polygon (or geometric shape) that	1. has three sides closed 2. has angles equaling 180 degrees 3. may be equilateral, isosceles, or scalene 4. may have acute, right, or obtuse angles 5. is the basis of the prism and the pyramid
		Add Other Appropriate Information

Figure 5.10

Defining Format Application

In addition to guiding students toward separating the category from the specific characteristics, Defining Format can serve the following writing and learning purposes:

■ Notetaking and Outlining—Students can use Defining Format's three-part structure to gather the essential elements of a word or term and then observe or analyze its components.

- Paragraph Development—Upon completing the three parts of this strategy to define a term, students can use the information to write the term's meaning in paragraph form. For example,

  A slave is a person who is owned by another person and is considered to be property that can be bought and sold. Slaves are generally unable to own their homes or belongings. They get their food, clothing, and shelter from their owners, but they work without wages and usually for long hours. Worst of all they do not have rights as parents and their children can be sold separately to other slaveholders.

- Comparing and Contrasting—After students have written definitions for two items belonging to the same category, they easily can compare the two items by matching characteristics that are similar or different. For example, after defining a triangle and a rectangle, students can write a paragraph by composing basic sentences that describe the corresponding characteristics for both objects. They follow the format outlined in the Defining Format visual organizer. Following is a student example showing the first few sentences that compare a triangle and a rectangle.

  We can compare a triangle with a rectangle. Both are polygons, but with different characteristics. A triangle has three sides that equal 180 degrees, while a rectangle is four-sided with angles equaling 360 degrees.

The compare/contrast aspects of Defining Format also can be used in conjunction with Venn diagrams and the "Double Bubble Maps" created by David Hyerle (1995). Double Bubble Maps are graphic organizers that can be used to help students visualize the relationship between two items belonging to the same category. These visual organizers can be used either before or after setting up Defining Format. By using the Venn diagram or the Double Bubble Map first, the students go from *picture to words*. As a follow-up activity, the students go from *words to picture*. Both strategies are important and offer students flexibility in thinking and constructing. Figure 5.11 shows a Venn diagram comparing a triangle and a rectangle. Figure 5.12 shows the same information in a Double Bubble Map.

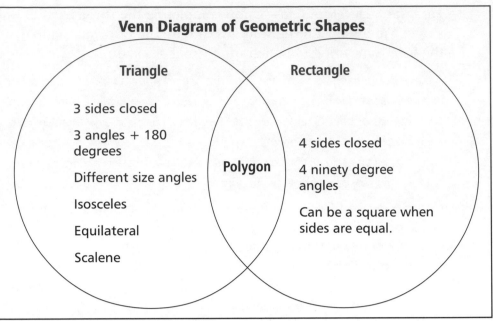

Figure 5.11

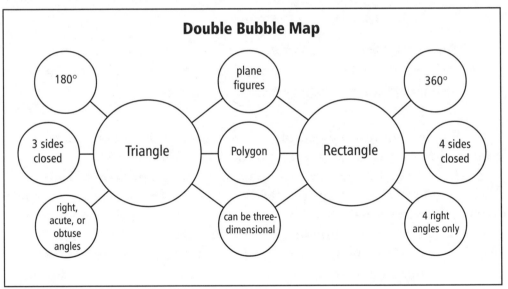

Figure 5.12

■ Expanded explanations—Each characteristic in the Defining
Format has the potential to be expanded as a detailed paragraph.
In writing about addition, for example, the student might elaborate on its first characteristic of requiring two or more numbers to
get a sum:

Any amount or type of number can be added. We can add four place numbers, fractions with the same or different denominators, negative and
positive numbers, prime numbers, and odd or even numbers. We always get
a sum, which is usually more than we started with, except when we add
negative numbers. Then we seem to get less.

TAXONOMY SHEET	
Object Categories	
A	art form
B	building
C	communication device, clothing, container
D	divider, dwelling
E	eating utensil
F	furniture, footwear, farm equipment
G	gemstone, geometric shape
H	headwear, habitat
I	illumination
J	jewelry
K	
L	
M	musical instrument, mineral, measuring device
N	number
O	opening
P	pictorial representation, partition
Q	
R	reference book, recording device
S	symbol, sports equipment, sailing vessel
T	timepiece, tool
U	
V	vehicle
W	writing tool, writing surface, window covering
X, Y, Z	

Figure 5.13

TAXONOMY SHEET	
Animal Categories	
A	amphibian, arachnid, arthropod, annelid
B	bird, biped, bovine
C	canine. cattle, carnivore. crustacean
D	domestic, dinosaur, diurnal, desert
E	equine
F	farm, feline, fish, fowl
G	grazing
H	herbivore
I	invertebrate, insect
J	jungle
K	
L	lepidoptera
M	mammal, mollusk, marsupial, mountain
N	nocturnal
O	omnivore, one-celled
P	primate, predator, pet
Q	quadruped
R	reptile, rodent, rain forest, ruminant
S	sea mammals
T	timberland
U	ungulate, ursurines
V	vertebrate
W	worm, woodland, water fowl
X	
Y	
Z	

Figure 5.14

By having students use Defining Format to define all subject-area terminology, they have a permanent template for organizing factual information that they can use for reports, presentations, and explanatory writing.

Some students may have difficulty citing the category for many of their terms. In such cases, it helps for the teacher to provide the students with category words. See Figure 5.13 for an example of a Taxonomy of Object Categories, Figure 5.14 for a Taxonomy of Animal Categories, and Figure 5.15 for a Taxonomy of Occupational Categories.

An additional way teacher can help students better understand categories is to set up a chart showing how a categorical term connects two related items (see Figure 5.16).

TAXONOMY SHEET

Occupational Categories

A	author, artist, athlete, actor
B	business tycoon, boxer
C	community helper, civil rights activist
D	doctor of medicine, dancer
E	entrepreneur, explorer
F	food preparer
G	general
H	health worker, horticulturist
I	investigator, illustrator
J	journalist
K	knight, king
L	legislator
M	musician, mountain climber
N	national leader, naturalist
O	opera singer, ornithologist, orator
P	poet, philanthropist, philosopher
Q	queen
R	religious leader
S	social activist, sculptor, scientist, social worker
T	teacher, talk-show host
U	union leader
V	veterinarian
W	writer, wrestler
X	
Y	youth leader
Z	zoologist

Figure 5.15

Categorial Terms as Connectors

Item	Category	Item
cup	container	bucket
cottage	dwelling	mansion
boot	footwear	sandal
rectangle	polygon	parallelogram
ruler	measuring device	meter stick
wall	partition	fence
flag	symbol	wreath
bat	sports equipment	hockey stick
dictionary	reference book	almanac
clock	timepiece	sundial

Figure 5.16

Using this chart, students can form the comparative statement; for example, "An almanac and a dictionary are both types of reference books, but contain different information." They can then set up their Defining Format for listing their shared and dissimilar characteristics.

Defining Format is the strategy that helps students write clearly and concisely on specific subject matter and to a "distant audience" that knows "very little." It also is a strategy that requires the student to organize through classification and to pay attention to the details that separate one item or concept from a similar item or concept. Finally, Defining Format allows students to write a cohesive paragraph with a clear opening statement and a support structure. From this strategy, students can backtrack to Taxonomies (for categories) and to Metacognition (for "I now know that I know . . .").

LINKING TO THE COMPUTER

Teachers may want to set up a file on classroom computer(s) with the Defining Format template, which students can access as needed. In addition, posting the Taxonomy of Categories will help students to complete their templates on the computer. Depending on the needs of the students, teachers also can provide Taxonomies of Categories to assist students in finding the categories of the terms they are defining.

Students can create their own books of Defining Formats with titles such as *Occupations from A to Z, The ABC Book of Animal Categories, Landforms and Waterways,* and so forth. These can be a combination of definitions with drawings for young students or full paragraph writings for older students. Another activity is to have students create their own glossaries for particular units that they then can use for review of important terminology.

CHAPTER 6

Profiles and Frames

Organizers for Writing

Begin with the end in mind.

—Stephen R. Covey

WHAT IS A PROFILE?

A Profile is a visual outline that helps the user organize information about a topic, such as animals, art, people of accomplishment, or political and geographic entities. Profiles allow students to select specific information from a detailed text and then recreate or write the information in their own words without resorting to straight copying. In fact, the only way that most people paraphrase, or write in their own words, is to take notes and then restate. By using Profiles, students learn the technique of writing it their way.

HOW TO USE PROFILES

Students can use Profiles to organize ideas prior to writing about them. Profiles can be set up by the teacher to highlight key information or to elicit a specific type of information. For example, if a teacher wanted students to learn about the primary characteristics of an animal, she or he could create a Profile requesting information on each of the desired characteristics, such as description, size, and sounds they make (see Figure 6.1).

Animal Profile

Directions: Select an animal that you like or that you are learning about and complete the following Profile. When you have all the information, write what you now know about that animal.

Name of Animal _____

Colors _____

Size _____

Special Markings (stripes, quills, spots, etc.) _____

Sound Animal Makes _____

Natural Habitats _____

_____

Food(s) Animal Eats _____

_____

Method of Getting Food _____

Method(s) of Movement _____

_____

Special Habits _____

_____

Classification (fish, amphibian, reptile, bird, mammal) _____

Other Classification (canine, feline, bovine, etc.) _____

Other Information

Figure 6.1

Figure 6.2 shows an Animal Profile created by a fourth grade student who used the textbook and the Internet to research her topic—Siberian tigers. Following this Profile is the student's written paragraph about the animal.

Animal Profile

Select an animal that you like or that you are learning about and complete the following Profile. When you have all the information, write what you now know about that animal.

Name of Animal   Siberian tiger

Colors   yellow orange

Size   Siberian tiger is 13 feet long and weighs about 700 pounds

Special Markings   thick yellow fur with dark stripes

Sound Animal Makes   loud roar and growl

Natural Habitat(s)   Northern Asia in the mountains and up to the Arctic Circle

Food(s) Animal Eats   deer, cattle, snakes, termites, and carrion (animals that have been lying dead for a while)

Method of Getting Food   hunting and preying (animal is a predator)

Method(s) of Movement   runs, walks, prowls

Special Habits   prefers to be alone, is solitary

Classification   mammal

Other Classification   belongs to the Feline family and is also known as Panthera tigris

Other Information   is very rare and endangered; the mother has a litter of two or three cubs and the cubs stay with the mother for about a year

Figure 6.2

My Report on the Siberian Tiger

The Siberian Tiger is the largest tiger in the world. It is thirteen feet long and weighs about seven hundred pounds. Its color is yellowy orange like other tigers and of course it has stripes on its thick fur. It lives in Northern Asia in Siberia, which is at the Arctic Circle, so the Siberian tiger is used to cold weather. The Siberian tiger is a mammal and also belongs to the feline or cat family.

This tiger is a predator. That means that it hunts other animals for its food. It will eat deer, cattle, snakes, and even termites. Sometimes it eats dead meat that has been lying around on the ground, called carrion. The Siberian tiger likes to be alone and only mates once a year with another tiger. When the mother has babies, she usually has two or three cubs and they stay with her for about a year. She teaches them to hunt so they can get their own food. The Siberian Tiger is endangered so we must not kill it or we will not ever be able to see this big tiger in person.

Profiles can be used to organize information in a variety of ways, for a multitude of subjects, and for writers at all grade levels. For example, the Animal Profile shown in Figure 6.1 can be adapted to a specific grade level, type of content, student interest, or other requirements. Following are just a few ways to adapt this Profile:

- Phylum, genus, and related species
- Method of reproduction and gestation period
- Weight, height, length, girth

Before completing a Profile, teachers can have students develop specialized Taxonomies, dealing with topics such as Animal Colors (e.g., amber, carmel, calico, pearl, salmon, tawny, umber, etc.) and Methods of Movement (e.g., bound, careen, dart, lumber, pounce, etc). These Taxonomies can provide the specialized vocabulary that relates to specific topics or concepts.

Teachers also may want to have students write Metacognitive Statements indicating prior knowledge of the topic. When the Profile is completed, students can add newly learned terms to their Taxonomies and revise their Metacognitive Statements (i.e., "I now know. . .").

Another option is for students to use the Profile as an outline and write a report using the information they gathered or researched. If students have been using the Defining Format strategy (see chapter 5) prior to completing a Profile (e.g., What is a tiger?), they can add the appropriate information from the Defining Format onto the Profile. Once students become familiar with Profiles, they can create their own, using familiar Profiles as models. By this interlocking of strategies, students reinforce their learning of the content and continuously develop and practice their writing skills.

Teachers can create Profiles for almost any aspect of their content area. For example, Profiles can be created about a planet, country, city, colony, cultural group, geometric shape, element or compound, and plant. Following are Profiles that focus on topics in different content areas: art, careers, and sports and games. These Profiles can be adapted or modified as appropriate to the teacher's curriculum needs.

Art Profile

To complete this template, students should be involved in a curriculum that presents various works of art: paintings, sculpture, photography, ceramics, or any other artistic form. Teachers may wish to use an Art Profile in conjunction with an Artist of the Month or Art Form of the Month program so that the students have ongoing opportunities to become familiar with different artists and their work. Students also could use this Profile to describe the artwork of their classmates. This personalization of art is particularly effective with young students who see themselves described as artists by their peers and whose artwork then is displayed with a completed Profile.

Art Profile

Directions: Select an art piece that interests you or that you are learning about and complete the Profile. When you have all the information, write about that piece of art.

Title of Art _____

Name of Artist _____

Years of Artist's Life _____

Type of Art _____

Size of Art _____

Year Completed _____

Place Where Art Can Be Seen _____

Owner or Donor of Art _____

Description of Art: _____

Subject or Theme: _____

Materials Used _____

Colors _____

Other Information _____

My Reaction to this Artwork:

_____

_____

_____

_____

_____

_____

_____

Figure 6.3

Career Profile

Directions: Select an occupation or career and use the Profile to record your information. You may obtain information by interviewing a person who has that career or you may check materials in the library or on the Internet. When you have completed the Profile, write a metacognitive statement that tells what you now know.

Name of Career or Occupation _____

Major Duties or Tasks _____

_____

Training Needed or Required _____

_____

Beginning Salary _____

Highest Range of Salaries _____

Personal Abilities Needed _____

_____

Places of Work (e.g., outdoor, indoors, foreign countries) ___

_____

Specializations within Career (e.g., gym teacher, police detective, technical writer) _____

_____

Other Information _____

_____

_____

_____

_____

_____

Figure 6.4

Career Profile

From the middle grades through high school, students need to learn about careers, especially those that can be related to their school studies. Students often ask, "Why do I have to know this?" and while not all topics are career related, students often get a broader view of the work world and the related academic or subject-area requirements when relationships are made.

Before completing a Career Profile, it helps for students to create a Taxonomy of Occupations. The Taxonomy can be a list of diverse occupations (e.g., author, baker, carpenter) or it can be a list of specialized occupations in relation to a specific subject (e.g., science: astronomer, biologist, cardiologist, ecologist, geneticist; mathematics: accountant, cartographer, economist, geographer, meteorologist, navigator). Students can choose a career from their Taxonomies to research, using the Profile for recording basic information.

Sports and Games Profile

Only occasionally does the health or physical education teacher ask students to write. An obvious reason is that students expect to *do* an activity, not write about it. Yet, the world of sports and games is full of writing—sports stories, instructions, events, awards, just to name a few. And since most students enjoy sports and games, they may enjoy and can come to enjoy writing about them. Prior to doing a Profile, students can create a Taxonomy of Sports and/or games. While this is an easy Taxonomy for students to do because of so much prior knowledge, research adds a new dimension. For example, there are sports that are not well-known in America, such as rugby, polo, and *jai alai*. Sports have histories, personalities, and specialized language that can interest and fascinate students.

Sports and Games Profile

Directions: Select a sport or game that interests you. Check books, magazines, and the Internet for information on that sport or game. When you have completed the Profile, write a sports article telling a person unfamiliar with the sport or game what she or he needs to know to understand it or play it.

Name of Sport or Game _____

Number of Players Required _____

Countries Where Popular _____

Equipment Needed _____

Uniform Items _____

Names of Team Positions (e.g., pitcher, goalie) _____

Scoring Terms _____

Other Special Terms _____

Object or Purpose (e.g., cross finish line first) _____

Other Information _____

Figure 6.5

WHAT IS A FRAME?

A Frame is similar to a Profile. Frames provide students with a structure for writing a story, an explanation, or a narrative. They are textual outlines that allow the student to get started and to focus on the topic through use of transition words or narrative markers. A Frame is useful as an instructional approach to guide students in the early stages of writing, such as sentence and paragraph development. When students use Frames, they begin to internalize the formal structures that writing demands and, over time, move to independent writing while retaining organization and a consistent point of view.

USING FRAMES

The types of Frames used can vary depending on grade level(s) and or subject area(s). Teachers can create their own or work with their students in forming the structure and deciding the information the Frame should contain. As a starter, here are several Frames that can be used repeatedly and with a wide range of grade levels and abilities. Teachers can modify them, it they wish, to meet their students' needs.

Frames for Primary Grades

Young students do particularly well when they use Frames as the springboard for organized and, eventually, detailed writing. Since many writers worry so much about spelling and format, they feel more secure when they have a plan to follow and know that their writing sounds "good."

Following is a Frame adapted from an old jump rope rhyme known as "A, My Name Is . . ."

E, my name is Evan,
My friend's name is Nora,
We come from Los Angeles,
And we like swimming.

Students can complete the Frame with a classmate and share their completed writing with the class.

After the students have completed the Frame, the teacher can assemble all of the Frames

---

A, My Name Is . . .

Directions: Complete this Frame by following your teacher's directions.

If you'd like, draw a picture of you and your friend.

Put the first letter of your first name in the box. ☐

My name is _____

My friend's name is _____

We come from _____

And we like _____

Figure 6.6

in a book that the students illustrate with drawings of themselves, their friends, and whatever else they might like. As an extension, the A, My Name Is Frame could be used to set up a Taxonomy of places the students come from as the start of a geography lesson or activity.

The following three Frames show the arrangement for eventual paragraph development and help the student separate ideas (see Figures 6.7–6.9). Teachers can use these samples as models to design their own Frames and make them more complex as their students' writing skills develop.

Meet My Teacher

My teacher's name is _____

She teaches me many things.

First, _____

_____

Second, _____

_____

Third, _____

_____

I think _____

_____

_____

Figure 6.7

Who Loves Me?

Many people love me.

First, _____

_____

Second, _____

_____

Third, _____

_____

These are some of the people who love me.

Figure 6.8

Then, Now, Later

Directions: Complete the first four lines of the Frame with important events that happened to you at different times in your life. Then complete the last two lines with what you think will happen when you grow up.

When I was small I _____

I also _____

Now I _____

I also _____

When I grow up I will _____

I will also _____

Figure 6.9

Frames for the Intermediate Grades, Middle and High School

Frames can be used to ensure that students can follow a writing plan, use transitional markers, and keep to the topic—the three essential rubrics of quality writing. When teachers ask their students to write without the assistance of Frames, students should be reminded to visualize the layouts of organized writing and to use appropriate transitions. An easy way to develop one's own Frames for content areas is to use the starting or topic sentences of books or texts the students are using. Then create the Frames that will allow students to write (in their own words) the significant information teachers want them to know. The following Frame could be started with a sentence in a social studies text: "Early people survived cold weather in several ways. First, _____. In addition, _____. Furthermore, _____."

A Frame using words from a mathematics text could use words similar to the following: "The Greeks demonstrated that no matter what the size and shape of a right triangle, certain relationships always held true. First, _____. From this concept, we find _____. Following this, we realize [discover, find out] _____."

When students then move from Frames to writing independently, they will have had intensive practice in fulfilling the basic rules of organization. Figures 6.10 through 6.13 show more detailed examples using starting or topic sentences in different content areas, including social studies and mathematics.

Fossils of Dinosaurs and Prehistoric Animals

How do we know so much about animals that roamed Earth millions of years ago?

Most of our knowledge comes from _____
_____

From this knowledge, we learn _____
_____

We also learn _____
_____

Finally we learn _____
_____

Fossils are found in many places.

They may be _____
_____

Another place to _____
_____

Sometimes fossils are found _____
_____

Fossils are formed in several ways.

Sometimes _____
_____

A second way _____

Then there are fossils that_____

By studying fossils, we better understand _____

Figure 6.10

People and Weather

People in different parts of the world have to adapt to different kinds of weather. They wear different clothing, have different types of houses, and eat different types of food.

In cold climates, for example, _____
_____
_____
_____

However, in climates that are warm all year round,
_____
_____
_____

People who live in places where the weather changes
_____
_____

Since I live in a place where the weather
_____,

I wear _____:
I live _____:

As for food, I am able to _____
_____

Because the earth has such varied climate, human beings have learned
_____
_____

Figure 6.11

Sculptures in Non–Western Cultures

There are many types of sculptures made by people in non–Western cultures.

Nomadic hunting groups, like the Inuit, have made _____ ,

_____, and _____

_____

Each of these sculptures have different purposes: For example, _____

_____. Then there is the ___

_____

Traditional African sculpture is very diverse. Among the Ashante _____

_____

In Nigeria, the Yoruba _____

_____

Further south, _____

_____

In the Far East, the religious teachings of Buddha influenced much art. There are statues of _____ that _____

Then there are buildings of worship in _____

_____

_____

Finally there are representations of different individuals who _____

_____

Figure 6.12

How to Add Fractions with Mixed Denominators

First, set up your fractions vertically. That means placing one number under the other.

Second _____

_____

_____

After that, _____

_____

_____

Then _____

_____

_____

Fourth _____

_____

_____

Finally, _____

_____

_____

If you have followed these steps, you will _____

_____

_____

_____

_____

Figure 6.13

LINKING TO THE COMPUTER

By making Profiles and Frames available on the computer, students can have ready access to easy response writing. Rather than having students "answer questions at the end of the chapter," they can paraphrase, restate, and compose original text that relates to the curriculum. Teachers may wish to create Frames for the computer from predictable books such as *Brown Bear, Brown Bear* (by Bill Martin) or *Strega Nona* (by Tomie DePaola) for students to improvise. Or teachers can create simple chronological Frames for historic events or the events of a person's life.

Profiles and Frames can be used to organize thoughts prior to writing biographies, autobiographies, and essays, and these uses are explained in chapters 7 and 8.

CHAPTER 7

Who's Who

Biographies and Autobiographies

We both exist and know that we exist, and rejoice in this existence and this knowledge.

—Saint Augustine

WHO'S WHO: THE HUMANITY IN WRITING

Who's Who is the strategy that combines Taxonomies, Profiles, Frames, and a variation of Defining Format (called Biographic Format) to guide students in writing the two exciting genres of biography and autobiography. By creating Taxonomies of mathematicians, social activists, inventors, and so forth, students have a research bank to draw upon. The Profiles, Frames, and Biographic Format serve as the organizational formats for this type of nonfiction writing. These two genres—biography and autobiography—are linked by similarities and differences that make both of them valuable for learning and for having in one's files or folders throughout the school years. Writing biographies and biographical sketches makes students focus on those persons who have contributed to a society's knowledge base, values system, technology, and apirations. Writing autobiographical pieces gets students to reflect upon their own history and their future goals and hopes.

Writers as young as kindergartners can use this strategy to write biographies. Biographies are commonplace topics for students of all ages as they learn about or commemorate famous people, or people of accomplishment. There is a greater interest today in learning about people whose contributions to humankind traditionally have been de-emphasized or overlooked. African Americans, Amerindians, and women are among those people who now get named or listed in textbooks along with the explorers of North and South America, presidents, and world leaders of the past and present. For generations, students have written biographic reports as they study history and current events.

An aspect of biographical learning often missing in the classroom is the focus on persons of accomplishment who have added to humankind's knowledge in subject areas. For example, how many mathematicians, except for Archimedes, Euclid, and Pythagoras, do students study in relationship to mathematics and then write about? Do students become acquainted with the great health professionals who have discovered cures and medicines for the dread diseases of the world? Who have been the dispensers of knowledge in biology, botany, geography, and other disciplines? Many students study facts and concepts about transportation or physical science without learning how motivated, creative human beings gathered the knowledge that is in today's texts and literature. As advocates for teaching about persons of accomplishment in all fields, the authors combine the previously described strategies with several new ones that, hopefully, will inspire students to emulate some of these people and to write about them in a variety of interesting ways.

FOCUS OF WRITING BIOGRAPHIES

The most important element in the biography of a person of accomplishment is her or his accomplishment or accomplishments. Yet, without guidance or strategies, many students write (or copy) a biography as a chronology—the person was born, went to school, got married, became a teacher of the deaf, and died! This type of writing is more like a newspaper insert for an obituary. The purpose of writing a biography is for the students to understand why they are celebrating that person and what the events or driving force(s) were that compelled the person to do the extraordinary or unusual.

By creating Taxonomies of mathematicians or social activists, for example, teachers can have class discussions prior to the writing that focus on questions such as "What makes someone a great mathematician?" or "Why were some women willing to give up personal and economic security to fight for the rights of other women?" Following discussions of issues such as these, students collect the names of those persons who rose to the top of their fields or society and then learn of their accomplishments or contributions, adding this information to their Profiles, Frames, and Biographic Format.

Setting Up Taxonomies for Biographical Writing

Early in the school year, teachers can plan with their students to keep ongoing Taxonomies of people related to the curriculum or subject areas. The names of these persons may come from texts, newspaper articles, library and Internet research, or students' prior knowledge. The taxonomies should be organized by related accomplishments, such as Women in the Arts or Great Amerindian Leaders. By having these Taxonomies posted or compiled in a notebook, students will become familiar with and knowledgeable about the vast humanity who have affected their lives.

Figure 7.1 is an example of a Who's Who Taxonomy that relates to mathematicians.

> *Example of student summary on Mathematicians of Magnitude:*
>
> Vladimir Kosma Zworykin was a Russian-born American physicist and mathematician who developed the television camera and picture tube. While he was a student at the Institute of Technology in St. Petersburg, Russia, he dreamed of coming to America to work in a research laboratory to study ways to improve radio communication. In 1929 he became director of the electronic Research Laboratory of Radio Corporation of America at Princeton, NJ, where he worked on television transmission and pictures. Later on he also helped develop a powerful electron microscope. All of us today who watch television are glad for the work of Vladimir Kosma Zworykin.
>
> *Seventh grade student*

Using Profiles for Biographical Writing

With the Who's Who Taxonomy serving as a data bank of names, students can select someone who interests them. Some students may read a full-length biography for information; others may use an article from an encyclopedia or the Internet. As they read or after they have read, the students need to extract the significant information that will allow them to write their piece, focusing on accomplishments and reasons for these accomplishments. The Profiles (see chapter 6) are the guides for getting this information, plus additional

TAXONOMY SHEET	
Mathematicians of Magnitude	
Find out as much as you can about these mathematicians who have contributed to our knowledge.	
A	Archimedes
B	Bernouli, Banneker, Bell, Boole
C	Cauchy
D	Descartes
E	Euclid
F	Fermat, Fibonacci
G	Galileo, Gauss, Galois, Grothendieck
H	Hypatia, Hilbert, Huntington
I	
J	Jacobi
K	Kepler, Kelvin, Kowalewska
L	Meitner, Mitchell, Mumford
M	Noether
N	
O	Pythagoras
P	
Q	
R	Riemann
S	
T	Steiner, Steinmetz
U	
V	
W	Weyl
X	
Y	
Z	Zworykin

Figure 7.1

information that relates to time periods and nationalities. Through such gathering of purposeful information, the students prepare themselves for writing a biographical sketch or report.

Figures 7.2 is a Profile for social and civil rights activists. This Profile can be adapted by the teacher or the students for biographies of people in a variety of other fields. Students should add other information that they consider important to the Profiles.

Profile for Social and Civil Rights Activist

Directions: Select a social or civil rights activist who interests you. Complete the profile. When you have all the information, write several paragraphs about that person.

Name of Activist _____

Years of Activist's Life _____

Nationality _____

Major or Significant Social Beliefs _____

_____

Accomplishments and Contributions to Humanity _____

_____

_____

_____

Publications _____

_____

Special Recognition and Rewards _____

_____

Other Information _____

_____

Figure 7.2

Figures 7.3 and 7.4 are examples of profiles students can use for preparation when writing biographical sketches about persons of accomplishment in mathematics and science.

Scientist Profile

Select a scientist who interests you. Complete the profile. When you have all the information, write several paragraphs about that scientist.

Name of Scientist _____

Years of Scientist's Life _____

Scientist's Nationality _____

Major Fields of Study (e.g., chemistry, astronomy, technology, etc.) _____
_____

Major Contributors to Science and Humanity

_____
_____
_____

Publications

_____
_____

Special Recognition and Rewards

_____

Other Information

_____

Figure 7.3

Mathematician's or Scientist's Personal Profile

Directions: Imagine that you are a scientist making a presentation at a scientific conference. Complete the following Personal Profile as the basis for introducing yourself and your work to your colleagues.

My Name _____
_____

My Place of Birth and My Early Schooling ___
_____

My College and University Studies and Training (or other training) _____
_____

My work was mainly influenced by the previous studies of _____
_____
_____

(Add other names if appropriate.)

In my own work, I contributed the following information (ideas):

_____

Figure 7.4

Using Frames for Biographical Writing

A Frame (see chapter 6) can be used as a tool to help students write a summary biographical sketch either to keep track of people they are studying or as the outline of a fuller report. Two very useful Frames for biographical writing are the Person of Accomplishment Frame and the Biography Frame. The teacher can post a copy of these frames in a visible area or give each student copies. The teacher also can make a template for using these Frames when writing by computer.

The Person of Accomplishment Frame (see Figure 7.5) is set up to state the subject's identity (i.e., name), define the subject's role (e.g., musician, mathematician, social activist), and describe the significant accomplishment that makes people celebrate or mark that person's life.

Example

The first sentence of this Frame guides the student in stating the person's *name* (i.e., Sally K. Ride), followed by the person's *identity* (astronaut) and continues with a *statement of accomplishment*.

Sally K. Ride was an astronaut who became the first American woman to become a crew member of the Challenger spacecraft in 1983 and travel into space.

The second sentence tells about the *person's dream, wish, or belief* that motivated the accomplishment.

She (Sally K. Ride) often thought about exploring the world outside Earth and

Person of Accomplishment Frame

Directions: Use this frame to write a summary biographical statement about a person of accomplishment.

_____ (Put in name) was a _____ (Put in identity of accomplishment) who

_____ (Put in significant accomplishment)

_____

She (He) believed (wanted, fought for, dreamed, hoped to)

_____

To accomplish her (his) goal(s) she (he)

_____

As a result of her (his) (dedication (hard work, beliefs, sacrifices)

_____

_____

(Put in the person's accomplishment(s)

_____

_____

Figure 7.5

> dreamed that she would be accepted into the NASA space program even though she was a woman.

The final sentence tells the *accomplishment or fulfillment* (or near fulfillment) of the dream

> As a result of her persistence, NASA changed its policy toward women and Sally K. Ride realized her dream of becoming the first American female astronaut.

By using this Frame, students have a simple way to keep track of and retain the essential information of well-known or accomplished people.

Another visual organizer or tool is Biographic Format (see Figure 7.6), which is similar to Defining Format (see chapter 5) but is designed for writing about a person rather than an object or concept.

BIOGRAPHIC FORMAT		
Who was Mary McLeod Bethune?		
Question	Identities	Accomplishments
Who was Mary McLeod Bethune? Mary McLeod Bethune was	an African-American educator who	1. believed that African-American girls needed a high-quality education 2. founded a boarding school for girls in Daytona, Florida, around 1910 3. merged her school with an all-male school to become Bethune-Cookman College 4. organized a training hospital for African-American nurses who had been denied access to white-only hospitals 5. became the director of the Office of Minority Affairs under Franklin D. Roosevelt, setting up schools for all minorities across America

Figure 7.8

Using this organizational form, students at almost all grade levels can add details within each main statement to develop expanded biographical reports. Here are two examples, one written by a third grade student on Sally K. Ride and the other written by a sixth grader on Mary McLeod Bethune.

Sally K. Ride was an astronaut who was the first woman to go into space. She was a crew member on the Challenger. Six women wanted to be in the space shuttle program, but only Sally K. Ride got into the program.

She always dreamed of being an astronaut. When she was a little girl she studied the planets and went to movies that showed people traveling from one planet to another. She pretended that she was a person like that and would make believe that she was the captain of a rocket ship.

Finally she got her wish on June 18, 1983. She was on a rocket called the -7 and rode into space for six days before coming back to Earth. If I were Sally K. Ride, I would feel very proud that I was the first woman to be allowed to be an astronaut.

Third grade student

Mary McLeod Bethune was an African-American educator who accomplished many things for African Americans and other minorities. She was especially interested in African-American girls because when she was living in the 1800s, African-American girls were not able to go to school. Since she was very poor herself when she was growing up, she knew how hard it was for other poor African-American girls. She decided to be a teacher in a girls' school and find a way to help poor girls come to her school.

In 1910 she moved from Chicago to Florida. She now had a little boy and she took him with her. When she was in Florida, she went everywhere asking people for money to help her start own school. A company named Procter and Gamble and a rich man named John D. Rockefeller thought she had a good idea and gave her money for a school that was called the Bethune Schools for Girls. By 1925 she had more than a hundred girls in her school and decided that now it would be better to have a school with boys and girls. So her school joined with Cookman Institute for a few years. A few years later the school which was a high school became a college called Bethune-Cookman College and Mary McLeod Bethune became the first president.

Sixth grade student

Expanding the Taxonomy for Elaboration and Details

As students prepare to write their biographies, they need to be aware of the identities (roles) of the persons about whom they are studying or writing. For example, Abraham Lincoln did not become a president until he had been a rail splitter, a reader, a lawyer, a debater, and so forth. He also had geographic and family identities (Kentuckian, husband). To help students understand the journey taken by their biographic subjects, they also should set up a Dual Taxonomy of Identities as illustrated in Figure 7.7. In this Taxonomy students first list the significant geographic, family, and occupational identities. And since many students have difficulty evoking words to describe the characteristics or traits of persons, they can use the Dual Taxonomy to compile a list of descriptive words for adding details to their topic sentences. Next, students select appropriate adjectives that match the identities of the person they are writing about (e.g., dynamic speaker). This Dual Taxonomy can then be used in conjunction with Profiles, Frames, or Biographic Format.

Many students have difficulty evoking words to describe the characteristics or traits of people and find themselves limited to words such as nice, kind, or good. By using a Dual Taxonomy, (see Figure 7.9), students can compile lists of descriptive words to add detail to their topic sentences.

As the following writing samples show, the adjectives enhance the identity in that the stated accomplishment is an expansion of the identity.

> Martin Luther King, Jr., was a forceful civil rights activist who was determined to improve the lives of African Americans and other minority peoples.

or

> Martin Luther King, Jr., was a magnificent orator whose speeches moved people to take action against laws of segregation and inequality.

USING WHO'S WHO TO WRITE AN AUTOBIOGRAPHY

An autobiography is a personalized biography, and therefore, many of the same strategies used for writing the biography can be used with adaptations. The autobiography does have its own specific genre format, however, in that the writer is working from a highly personal perspective.

TAXONOMY SHEET
Person of Accomplishment: Martin Luther King, Jr.

Directions: Use an Identity and Characteristics Taxonomy to write a report about Martin Luther King, Jr. You may use the Biographic Format or the Person of Accomplishment Frame as a template or structure to help you write your report.

	Identity	Characteristics
A	American	admirable
B		brave
C	civil rights activist	capable, caring
D		determined
E	educator	energetic
F	father	forceful
G	Georgian	generous
H	humanitarian	humane
I		intelligent, independent
J		judicious
K		kind, knowledgeable
L	leader	loyal
M	minister	magnificent
N	Nobel Prize winner	noble
O	orator	open-minded
P	peacemaker	peaceful
Q		
R		reasonable
S	southerner, speaker	sympathetic
T	teacher	thoughtful
U		understanding
V		valiant
W	writer	wise
X		
Y		
Z		zealous

Figure 7.7

Here, too, students can create Taxonomies. However, the Taxonomies will be related to themselves, with topics such as My Interests and Hobbies, My Favorite Authors, Places I Would Like to Visit, among others. Again, the Taxonomy is the database, or data bank, that provides information for the personal Profiles, which teachers and students can create together. From the Profiles, the students can move to a variety of Frames that are organized around personal themes or topics (e.g., memories, feelings, wishes).

Students generally enjoy writing about themselves, and thus, students at all grade levels can write autobiographies. One way to get started is to have students create a Personal Identity Taxonomy at the beginning of the school year as described in chapter 2. After the students have their individual Personal Identity Taxonomy, they complete the Personal Profile. With these two preliminary items, they can create both short and long pieces about themselves, adding information each year and building for themselves an ongoing story of their lives. Students can use a Personal Profile (see Figure 7.8) to help them create a valuable record of who they are and what they hope to become.

Personal Profile

Directions: Use this profile to write information about yourself. When the profile is completed, write a description of yourself or use the profile for information in your autobiography.

First Name _____ Middle Name _____

Last Name _____ Other Names _____

ADDRESS (for local and interplanetary use)

Street Number _____ Street(Avenue, Road, Lane, Circle, etc.) _____

Borough, Village, Town, or City _____

State _____ Zip Code _____ Country _____

Continent _____ Hemisphere _____

Planet _____

BIRTH INFORMATION

Date of Birth _____ Place of Birth _____

Present Age _____

(continued)

Figure 7.8

PHYSICAL DESCRIPTION

Height _____ Weight _____ Color of Eyes _____

Color of Hair _____

Other Physical Characteristics (Curly Hair, Tall, Dark, Blond, etc.)

_____

PERSONAL INTERESTS

Sports I Enjoy _____

My Favorite Television Programs _____

_____

Movies I've Enjoyed _____

_____

Music I Play and/or Music I Like _____

_____

My Singing and Dancing Activities _____

_____

SCHOOL INFORMATION

School I'm Attending _____

Schools I Have Attended _____

My Best School Subjects _____

_____

My After-School Activities _____

_____

My Memorable Teachers _____

Other Information about Me _____

_____

_____

Figure 7.8 (continued)

FRAMES FOR AUTOBIOGRAPHIES

An autobiography is not only a record of one's past but an ongoing
endeavor that the writer uses to document events for future retrospec-
tion. The student who has been fortunate enough to have written anecdotes, feelings, beliefs, dreams, and other information about himself or
herself has a personal gift for future sharing with his or her family and
family-to-be and the makings of a complete autobiography or memoir.
Figures 7.9–7.16 are frames that can guide students in writing their
autobiographies and that can be used in a wide range of grade levels
from primary through secondary. These Frames can be used by teachers
either as models for creating Frames specific to the needs of their classrooms or used as is.

Memories

I am now _____ years old and I can remember many important
events.

I remember the first time I

Then I remember when

When I was _____ years old, I

This year, when I started _____ grade, I

I know that next year

Figure 7.9

Memories Over Time

My life has had many events from the time I was born until now. Here are some highlights that I would like to share.

First there were my early years, from my birth till I went to school. (Write several events.)

When I started school, there were many events and changes in my life.

I also have memories of my family and my family life.

I am now looking ahead and thinking of my future.

Figure 7.10

Down Memory Lane

Think back to important events in your life and complete each sentence. Then add the details of that memory to the sentence.

One of my earliest memories is

_____

One of my happiest memories is

_____

One of my most exciting memories is

_____

In addition, I have other memories that I would like to share.

_____

Figure 7.11

My Accomplishments—From Then to Now

Although I am only _____ years old, I can look back on many accomplishments in my life.

When I was a preschooler I already knew how to _____,

_____, and _____.

By the time I entered school, I could _____,

_____, and _____.

During my early school years, I _____,

_____, and _____.

At this time of my life, I can _____,

_____, and _____.

Having accomplished so much already, I know that I will be capable of
_____, _____, and

_____.

Figure 7.12

Feelings

Like all people, I have many feelings, some pleasant and some unpleasant. Here are some of my feelings that I would like to share.

I laugh when

_____

I get angry when

_____

I feel great when

_____

I worry when

_____

I feel I have had a good day when

_____

Figure 7.13

If I . . .

Complete these sentences. Then go back to each sentence and write three or four sentences telling more about what you *would* do to make what you *could* do happen.

If I could do one great act in my life, I _____

If I could honor a wonderful person, I _____

If I could travel to any place I wanted, I _____

If I could help people in need, I _____

If I could entertain one person of accomplishment, I _____

_____

Figure 7.14

I Have a Dream

Use the frame to write your dream of the future. You probably have more than one dream, so use this frame as often as you like to express your ideas. Your dream might be about your personal life or about how you might help others.

I have a dream that _____

In this dream, I see myself _____

To make this dream come true, I _____

_____

_____

Figure 7.15

Twenty Years from Now

Imagine yourself twenty years from now and complete this frame. Then add details to each sentence.

Twenty years from now, I will be _____ years old.

I expect to have _____

I might be living _____

Hopefully, I will have a job or career as _____

_____

As I look ahead to twenty years from now, I know that _____

_____

Figure 7.16

LINKING TO THE COMPUTER

The templates for these Taxonomies, Profiles, and Frames can be created in word processing programs so they can be stored on disk or the computer and made available to students either to print out or use only electronically. Teachers can modify or add to these formats to meet their own students' needs. Even more valuable, students can create their own Taxonomies, Frames, and Profiles so that they gain insight into what they feel is significant and record what they want to write about.

CHAPTER 8

Reasons, Causes, Results

The Essay—Personal, Persuasive, Explanatory

> *You often need to write in order to have anything to say.*
>
> —Frank Smith

REASONS, CAUSES, RESULTS: THE BASIS OF THE ESSAY

"Write an essay of 250 words about. . . ." What high school or college student hasn't heard those words? And what student hasn't pondered over what exactly an essay is. The *Random House Unabridged Dictionary* defines *essay* as "a short literary composition on a particular theme or subject, usually in prose and generally analytic, speculative, or interpretative." Yet, even this definition doesn't necessarily help the student writer understand the required format or know quite what the teacher has in mind without being given a detailed explanation. Once students have a clear definition of what an essay is and a strategy or plan for writing essays, however, they begin to write clearly and pointedly.

Based on the topics most teachers assign, there are three major categories of the essay format that students need to be taught: personal, persuasive, and explanatory (sometimes called expository). Each of these essay types can begin or contain the explicit phrase *There are three reasons why*. This phrase can then be transformed into *There are (or were) three causes (or three results)*. By understanding the differences in the three types of essays and in using the phrase *There are three reasons why*, students have a starting strategy for essay writing that can be expanded and elaborated upon. In general, three is an adequate or reasonable number to explain an idea, although students may want to write several reasons or causes. The num-

taxonomies

*composing with
keywords*

metacognition

defining format

*profiles
and frames*

who's who?

**reasons, causes,
results**

*where in
the world*

premises, premises

quotable quotes

*personifications
and interactions*

*morphology,
etymology,
and grammar*

ber of reasons is optional and dependent upon the level and ability of the writer.

In the personal essay, the student writes from the personal perspective, analyzing, speculating, or interpreting from that perspective. However, when students do not receive adequate instruction on how to write this type of essay, they often wander off the topic or find they have "nothing to say." Further, without instruction and practice in writing the personal essay, they have even greater difficulty in mastering the persuasive or the explanatory essay, which requires the writer to cite arguments—pro and con—and use research to back up opinions and explain concepts.

In the persuasive essay, the students express a belief or point of view that they want others to share with them. This type of essay traditionally uses the editorial *we* to suggest or imply that others share the same opinion. The persuasive essay writer then speaks for her or his constituents or group and uses several arguments to influence or optimally win over the opposition or the unconvinced.

In the explanatory essay, the writer is less likely to express a personal point of view than in the personal essay, but rather objectively explains the why or how of a particular concept or event. The explanatory essay focuses on factual information and thus lends itself to all content areas. It is a common writing assignment in schools, particularly at the secondary level.

Begin with the basic essay format, illustrated below, from which the students can build a repertory of essay writing. The basic format always begins with "There are (were) three reasons (causes, ways, results, purposes)."

The Basic Essay Frame: Three Reasons

Writers should think in terms of at least *three* of any of the following when they are asked to write an essay.

- Three reasons
- Three causes
- Three ways
- Three results
- Three purposes

Then use an arrangement of transition words to move from one paragraph to the next.

- First or Most important
- Second, In addition, Following that, Furthermore
- Last, Finally, Above all

Always conclude by restating what you said in the opening sentence or paragraph.

The Look of a Basic Essay

- Opening statement. May have two or three detail sentences to clarify opening statement.
- First reason, cause, result, etc. Add three to four detail sentences supporting first statement.
- Second reason, cause, etc., with detail sentences.
- Third reason, cause, etc., with detail sentences.
- Concluding sentence. May have one or two detail sentences.

Personal Essays

After the teacher has explained the format of a basic essay, she or he can then introduce the personal essay, which generally is one of the easier essays for students to write. It is not likely to require research or background reading and can almost always be written in a short period of time. In this type of essay, the student writes from the personal perspective, analyzing, speculating, or interpreting from that perspective.

Prompts for a personal essay generally take the form of an invitation to write about something of personal interest to the writer, such as the following topics:

- Write about a person who has influenced your life.
- Tell about an exciting adventure you had on a trip with your family.
- Think of a place you would like to visit and tell why.
- Imagine what your life would be like if you were five inches tall.
- Write an essay telling why you think the United States should or should not bomb (name of place).

Figure 8.1 shows a writing assignment for a personal essay using a Taxonomy and Frame.

A useful way for students to organize the ideas related to the three key ideas, or "three reasons," is to organize their essays on three sheets of paper, with each reason on a separate page. They now have the outline, or what can be termed a summary essay statement. At the inception of this strategy, students write at least three summary essay statements in which they are able to come up with *major* reasons, as illustrated in the following examples of student writing.

There are three reasons why I admire Harriet Tubman.
First she helped her own people get free.
In addition, she came up with a good idea called the Underground Railroad.
Finally, she made sure that her son would never be a slave.
These are the reasons why I admire Harriet Tubman.

Second grade student

There are three reasons why I am planning for college now.
First, I know that I must have good grades all through school so I could get into a good college like Duke or Michigan.
In addition, I will need a lot of money for college, so I have to start saving money now.
Finally, I want to get a basketball scholarship and to do that I must become the best player on my team.
For these reasons I am planning for college now.

Sixth grade student

Every morning when I wake up and look at the housing project where I live, I dream of taking a bicycle trip to Utah. I have three good reasons for this dream. First, my friend told me that Utah has the most beautiful mountains in the United States and since I've never been to the mountains, this is where I want to go. In addition, my friend said that there are many bicycle paths that twist up and down and make riding lots of fun and exciting. Finally, I'm tired of riding my bicycle in traffic where there are always trucks and taxis and people in your way. I'm sure Utah is not like that at all. I think these are very good reasons for dreaming about a bicycle trip in Utah.

Ninth grade student

TAXONOMY SHEET
Instructions to Students

Many times you will need to write a personal essay in which you tell why you believe an idea or enjoy an activity or admire a particular person. Below is a Taxonomy of words you might need to write a personal essay beginning with the words, "There are three reasons why I . . ."

A	admire
B	believe
C	care about
D	dream
E	expect, enjoy
F	feel
G	
H	hope
I	intend
J	
K	
L	love, like
M	might
N	need
O	
P	plan, prefer
Q	
R	
S	
T	think
U	understand
V	
W	wish, want
X	
Y	
Z	yearn for

Figure 8.1

Once students have mastered this format, they have a template for all personal essays. The student who wrote the summary outline on Harriet

Tubman went back and added details to each page. On the first page, she elaborated on how Tubman helped slaves reach freedom.

> Harriet Tubman would secretly meet with other slaves in the woods. She would teach them songs that gave directions of where they should go. She also taught them how to make signals with their hands so that only slaves would know what the signals meant. Many slaves were scared about getting caught, but Harriet Tubman told them to be brave.

Persuasive Essay

The personal essay is the springboard for the persuasive essay. In the persuasive essay, the writer may state her or his opinion or serve as the spokesperson for a group that wants to convince others to take action or take a specific position on a particular topic. The writer must clearly and positively state the position or point of view and then provide convincing arguments for that point of view. The conventional opening phrase for the persuasive essay is "We should. . . ." In a persuasive essay, the writer uses *we*, rather than *I* to make the audience believe that he or she represents a consensus. The word *should* is used to emphasize the significance of the belief or issue. Students can have the option of using *need to, must, have to,* or similar words that are meant to convince.

The format is similar to that of the personal essay, with the exception of the opening and concluding sentences. Since the persuasive essay advocates a cause or states a belief, it is a popular school genre and a necessary social genre. Following are a sampling of topics that lend themselves to persuasive writing. Of course, teachers will have their own, and students should search for topics that allow them to express their beliefs.

There are three reasons why we should . . .

- Keep the environment free of pollution
- Exercise every day
- Eat an abundance of fruits and vegetables
- Find homes for the homeless
- Give to our favorite charity
- Visit senior citizens who are homebound
- Keep our bodies free of drugs and tobacco

Following are three examples of persuasive writing from first, fourth, and tenth grade students, all on the same topic but with different levels of depth.

There are three reasons why we should eat lots of vegetables. First, vegetables have vitamins like vitamins A, B, C, and D. A second reason is that vegetables are good for your blood and your bones. A third reason is that you will feel strong and healthy. So even if you don't like how vegetables taste, you still should eat them for the reasons I said.

First grade student

There are three reasons why we should eat vegetables. First, all vegetables have many vitamins and minerals that help you get strong bones and good teeth. Second, vegetables help you have better digestion and you won't have so many stomach aches. Last, vegetables can even taste good especially if you eat them in a salad with a good salad dressing and bread sticks. So listen to me and eat your vegetables.

Fourth grade student

Doctors, health teachers, and dietitians are all telling us that we should eat more vegetables and less meat. Here are their reasons. First, they say that many vegetables like broccoli and Brussels sprouts contain antioxidants that can help prevent cancer. Then, there are vegetables such as kale and collard greens that give us calcium for strong bones and teeth. A third important reason is that vegetables provide our bodies with fiber to make our digestive system work better. If we want to have healthy lives we need to listen to doctors, health teachers, and dietitians who are telling us to eat more vegetables.

Tenth grade student

Explanatory Essay

The third type of essay based on three reasons is the explanatory essay. In this type of essay, the writer uses an opening sentence beginning with the words, "There are three reasons why," followed by the topic itself, as in "There are three reasons why the world is facing global warming."

The writer of an explanatory essay generally takes a neutral position and provides the reader with factual information with little, if any, opinion. This type of essay almost always requires research and substantiation of information. It is the genre most frequently found in textbooks and academic writing. Explanatory essays are used to write about various topics and lend themselves to all content areas. Following are suggested prompts for several different content areas that teachers can use as models to create their own prompts.

There are three reasons why . . .

- The American colonists rebelled against King George
- Cities often are built close to a river
- Shakespeare's plays are still enjoyed today
- The English Navy defeated the Spanish Armada

Here is an example of a middle school student's writing about the Spanish Armada from material researched on the Internet.

> In 1588 Spain had the strongest navy in the world and was the world's most powerful country. King Philip II of Spain thought that if his navy could beat the English Navy, Spain would control all of North America as well as South America. He gathered 130 ships with 300,000 men that set sail for England. He put Alonso Perez Guzman, his best commander, in charge of the fleet and was sure that his ships would win against the English. But for three major events that King Philip couldn't foresee, the English Navy was able to defeat the Spanish Armada.
>
> First, English spies found out about the plan and the English Navy attacked the Spanish Navy, damaging so many ships that the Spanish navy had to wait another year before it could set sail again. Then in July 1588, the Spanish Armada headed for England, but now the English navy was much stronger and they attacked again. They sank many Spanish ships and forced other ships to go back to a port in France. Third, came an attack by the English led by Lord Howard. This time, the English sent out special fire ships that made the Spanish sailors panic and get separated from the other ships. By breaking apart, the English navy was able to destroy fifty-four of the 130 ships. Spain was too poor to build another navy, so England became ruler of the seas. These three significant naval events allowed the English to get control of North America and begin its settlements of the colonies and Canada.
>
> *Eighth grade student*

Expanding the Essay

After students can comfortably write personal, persuasive, and explanatory essays, they can be shown how to use the same format for explaining causes and results. This extension into causes and results is particularly valuable for writing in all the content areas.

In science, students might need to write a personal essay telling the results of an experiment or the causes of an earthquake. In mathematics, students might write a personal essay telling the results of a survey or a building project. Social studies teachers particularly focus on causes and results to understand the immediate and underlying causes of a war or the results of agreements and treaties. Figure 8.2 is a plan that uses a combination of strategies for studying the immediate and underlying causes related to historical actions or events as well as their results. It outlines the essential information the students need to know to understand why wars begin, what happens during the war, and what results from the war.

By organizing the information this way, the students can use all of the writing strategies that have been introduced so far, adding now the strategies for "causes and results." Students learning about the American Revolution can create several Taxonomies: names of prominent American leaders; British opponents; American and British generals; battles and their locations, and perhaps others. The students might have set up a chronology of events leading up to the war and another chronology of events leading to victory over the British. Some students might have used Defining Format and Biographic Format to answer questions such as "What is a revolution?' "What was the Declaration of Independence?' and "Who was John Adams?" On a regular basis, they should be writing brief metacognitive statements that indicate growing knowledge and understanding of the war. With this continuous practice, students will be writing in greater depth, citing reasons, causes, and results. Below are examples of opening statements written by students at intermediate and secondary levels on the topic of the American Revolution.

How to Study a War

In studying about a war, you will need to understand and write about the following aspects of this unfortunate human behavior. You will need to set up Taxonomies and write metacognitive statements telling what you have learned or what you know you understand. Use Defining Format for all new terminology and Biographic Format for important leaders and heroes in the war. Write personal, persuasive, and explanatory essays relating to causes, outcomes, and results. Following are the aspects of war you need to study and write about:

- Combatants or opponents

- Underlying causes of the war

- Immediate causes

- "Players"—leaders, generals, heroes

- Significant battles

- Outcomes of the war

- Aftermath or results

Figure 8.2

There were three major underlying causes for the American Revolution. First, the colonists were angry at King George for making them pay taxes without their consent. Second, many colonists wanted to settle in lands west of the colonies and were stopped by British laws. Finally, American shipbuilders and traders did not want to be controlled by British ship owners and merchants.

There were three important results that came from the writing of the Declaration of Independence. For the first time, the thirteen colonies acted together and agreed upon separating from England. Then the writers of the Declaration wrote inspiring words that had not been said before like "All men are created equal," and all people are entitled to "life, liberty, and the pursuit of happiness." Most important, the Declaration of Independence made the colonists think of themselves as being Americans instead of British. These are the results that are most meaningful to me.

Even though George Washington and his men suffered from cold and hunger at Valley Forge, their suffering had good results for the American Revolution. One result was that the colonists admired George Washington for his courage and wanted him to win more than ever before. Another result was that the Continental Congress was able to raise more money from the colonists and then from France to help General Washington. The third result was that George Washington made sure that his men were better prepared with food and clothing for the next winter. So even though George Washington and his men had a terrible winter in Valley Forge, there were good results that came later.

The explanatory essay is also important in explaining and clarifying ideas and concepts in science, as illustrated in the following explanatory paragraph on genetics by a high school student studying genetics.

There are three types of traits that humans inherit: physical, biochemical, and behavioral. The physical traits are those that relate to resemblances to parents such as height, weight, hair and eye color, body shapes, and so forth. The biochemical traits that humans inherit can be blood types, bone structure, and a tendency towards certain diseases or sicknesses. The behavioral traits, such as intelligence, aggression, or gentleness, may be both inherited or learned. For example, scientists are not always sure whether intelligence is a behavior that we inherit or we learn, or maybe it's both inherited and learned. I will now explain these three traits in detail.

In a high school mathematics class, a student explained the history of algebra by starting with an organizing sentence that stated how he would structure his paragraph.

The history of algebra can be divided into three distinct periods. First algebra developed in the ancient civilizations of Egypt, Babylon, Greece, Persia, and Arab lands. The next stages of development took place during the Renaissance, mainly in Italy and France. The modern phase started late in the 18th century with discoveries and theorems of mathematicians from Germany, Great Britain, and the United States.

While students may want to or may need to use other formats, the simplicity of the essay formats described here give students an easy way to express complex ideas. The starting sentences also prepare the reader for what to expect and allow the writer to set up detailed, informative paragraphs. When students so often are told to render previously written text "in their own words," the structure of Three Reasons, Three Ways, Three Causes, or Three Results provides a dependable system for clear writing.

LINKING TO THE COMPUTER

In previous years, when students wrote essays, their companion was the encyclopedia. Today, it is the Internet. That is good news and bad news. The good news (for the students) is that they no longer have to "copy the encyclopedia." The bad news is, of course, that the students may not see any purpose in writing if all the information they need has already been written and is easily printed out. Yet, writing in one's own words does bring a sense of accomplishment, and students do like their voice to be heard. By providing them ways to write personal, persuasive, and explanatory statements, and with the word processor as a tool, the students have a viable way of reforming and restating and thereby absorbing and learning new material. With these basic starters, students can reorganize or extract the ideas from text information and recreate the information in their own words to reflect their own ideas or knowledge.

CHAPTER 9

*W*here in the World

Locating Our Writing

A client of a travel agent called inquiring about a travel package to Hawaii. After going over all the cost information, the client asked, "Would it be cheaper to fly to California and then take the train to Hawaii?"

From an Internet posting at www.jokes2go.com

WHERE IN THE WORLD: A STRATEGY FOR LOCATION AND SETTING

The strategy Where in the World combines teaching the students an organizational system of geographic locations with the strategies of Taxonomies, Metacognition, Defining Format, and Reasons, Causes, Results. The organizational system is based on the geopolitical concept that much of the world currently consists of political divisions (streets, cities, towns or villages, counties, and countries), entities created by humans, and natural divisions (continents, hemispheres, planets, and galaxies), and entities resulting from forces of nature. These geopolitical or geographic terms often are difficult for students to understand, and many times textbooks use these terms without clear, or without any, definition, assuming that students (and teachers) know exactly what a country or a city is. Yet, students need to grasp the distinction between political and natural divisions in order to know where they live or in order to understand the history of exploration, settlements, immigration, war, and their own families' lives.

Geography as Knowledge

Everybody and everything has to be someplace. An almost ridiculous statement, yet, with the exception of social studies, most school subjects are taught with no, or very little, reference to geography. In fact, geography is rarely taught as a separate subject in most schools, and many students, even in middle school, are uncertain about terms such as city, state, country, or continent, and often do not know *exactly* where they live. In New York City, for example, fifth graders who live in the Bronx might guess that the Bronx is a state, a country, the street where they live, and occasionally a continent, rather than a borough of the city of New York.

In the preface to *Cultural Literacy,* E. D. Hirsch, Jr., refers to America's "lack of cultural literacy," a term that he uses to mean the "possession of the basic knowledge needed to thrive in the modern world" (1987, xiii). In his controversial lists of what he believes students need to know, Hirsch cites dozens of geographic references that he says most American high school students would be unable to locate either on a map or simply by telling where the places are. How many students, he asks, could readily locate the Alamo, Appomattox, Gettysburg, Seneca Falls, or Valley Forge?

IMAGINING WHERE IN THE WORLD FOR TEACHING WRITING

Many teachers today feel overwhelmed with the vast content of material they are required to teach beyond subject areas—from drug abuse to computer literacy to conflict resolution. These extra teaching burdens leave the teacher with little time to stop and point out or explain geographic information. Often there is a lack of integration of geography or geographical terms and places among subjects so that the science teacher who mentions Gregor Mendel's experiments with pea plants in Austria may not mention or think about locating Austria or any other place where scientific study has taken place. The mathematics teacher, having to cover so much material, may feel put upon if she or he has to stop and tell where Rome was when explaining Roman numerals or where the Arabs traveled to when they discovered or invented "Arabic" numbers, especially the zero. The language arts teacher, too, may not want to stop to discuss the geography of Hannibal in *Tom Sawyer* or the Canadian North Woods in the story *Hatchet* in the pressure to get through the reading.

Yet, with awareness of the need for improving students' sense of location and geography and with the continuous implementation of the writing strategies previously introduced, students can develop an in-depth knowledge of where in the world they are and where in the world the knowledge they are acquiring comes from. With Taxonomies of geographic information, Defining Format for defining geographic terms, Who's Who for learning about people of accomplishment in exploration and discovery, essays about Reasons and Causes related to geography, and now, Where in the World for the integration of geography into all their writing, students can become geographically literate.

Teachers can introduce the concept of place when students first enter school by making sure students know their street address (e.g., 122 Cloverdale Road), their borough, town, or city (Albany), county, and their state (New York). With this information in place, teachers can ask students (hopefully by second grade) how they would tell "their address to a Martian." Teachers can explain that during the twenty-first century, Earthlings may need to correspond with Martians and others in outer space and; thus, they will need to know their complete address, that might look something like this:

> 22 Hunters Lane (my street)
> Coconut Creek (my town)
> Florida (my state)
> United States of America (my country)
> North America (my continent)
> Western Hemisphere (my hemisphere)
> Earth (my planet)
> Milky Way (my galaxy)

From this format, the student writes up a simple statement:

> 22 Hunters Lane is my street. Coconut Creek is my town. Florida is my state. The United States of America is my country. North America is my continent. The Western Hemisphere is my hemisphere. The Earth is my planet. The Milky Way is my galaxy.

The teacher can point out to the students that street, town, state, and country are called *political divisions* and continent, hemisphere, planet, and earth are *natural divisions*. These terms—*political division* and *natural division*—will be used later when the students create Defining Formats and need to determine the categories for these terms.

Figure 9.1 is a Defining Format used to compare two geographical concepts: a country and a state of the United States.

DEFINING FORMAT
What is a Country?

Question	Category	Characteristics
What is a country? A country is a	political division that	1. is independent, sovereign, or self-govern-ing 2. has borders with other countries 3. may be governed by a president, monarch, prime minister, chancellor, or dictator 4. has its own army or defense system 5. may issue its own currency 6. has one or several main languages 7. has shared customs and culture

What is a State (in the U.S.)?

Question	Category	Characteristics
What is a state? A state is a	political division that	1. is dependent upon the U.S. government 2. has borders with other states 3. is governed by a governor 4. does not have its own army or defense system, but may have a state militia 5. may not issue its own currency 6. has one government language, though other languages may be used by the population 7. may have shared customs and culture

Figure 9.1

Defining Format lays out the similarities and differences between two political divisions, in this case that of the United States and the individual state. These comparisons can be extended to cities, or in the case of other countries to provinces. Teachers can add other characteristics, but these characteristics become less significant than the first or primary characteristic.

Along with Defining Format, students can create and complete Profiles. Profiles provide students with a template for focusing on information related to a specific topic or subject. From the Profile rendered as Figure 9.2, students can create narratives and reports on the personal geography and on the political and natural entities or divisions. Students will find the use of Reasons, Causes, Results especially helpful in their geographic writing.

SkyLight Professional Development

From the Profile shown in Figure 9.2, students can create or work on other Profiles as they learn about either their local communities or their town or city. In studying about cities, students will notice that many cities grow up around rivers. From this observation, students can write explanatory pieces that tell how rivers and cities interrelate and how people in cities depend upon and use rivers for their work and recreation. This topic is important from as early as second or third grade through high school. Many students have seen rivers (both small and large) and are eager to know where they start and where they end or why they are clear or muddy or dry up or overflow. A field trip to a local river can be a good starting point for asking questions and making observations. As students move through the grades, they will discover how almost every major city of the world is on a river. Following are suggested writing topics, while Figure 9.4 shows a River Profile.

- There are three important reasons why many major cities of the world are located on rivers.

- I would like to explore the _____ River for these three reasons.

- We need to take care of our rivers for the following reasons.

- There are many ways that people benefit from living near a river.

Personal Geography Profile

Set up your own personal geography page by filling in as many of these items as you can.

My Birthplace _____

My Mother's Birthplace _____

My Father's Birthplace _____

Birthplaces of My Grandparents:

Maternal Grandmother _____

Grandfather _____

Paternal Grandmother _____

Grandfather _____

Places I Have Lived _____

_____

States I Have Visited

_____

Cities in the United States I Have Visited or Lived in

_____

Countries and Cities Outside of the United States I Have Visited or Lived in

_____

Places I Would Like to Visit

_____

Figure 9.2

TAXONOMY SHEET

Cities and Their Rivers

Select a city from below or any other one that you would like to know about. Create a brochure that tells the sites and activities that you would see along the river of that city.

A	
B	Buenos Aires/La Plata, Baghdad/Tigris and Euphrates, Budapest/Danube
C	Cairo/Nile, Calcutta/Ganges, Cincinnati/Ohio, Cologne/Rhine
D	
E	Edinburgh/Clyde
F	
G	
H	Hamburg/Elbe
I	
J	
K	
L	London/Thames, Lyons/Rhone
M	Montreal/St. Lawrence, Minneapolis/Mississippi
N	New York/Hudson, New Orleans/Mississippi
O	Omaha/Platte
P	Paris/Seine, Pittsburgh/Allegheny
Q	
R	Rome/Tiber
S	St. Louis/Mississippi, Stratford/Avon, Shanghai/Yangtze St. Paul/Mississippi
T	
U	
V	Volgograd/Volga, Vienna/Danube
W	Warsaw/Vistula
X	
Y	
Z	

Figure 9.3

The City Profile (see Figure 9.5) can be a follow-up activity after the River Profile or it can be done by itself.

From the examples of Profiles, students can create or work on other Profiles as they learn about their local communities, towns, or cities. Following are writing prompts for a unit on cities or a specific city:

■ Three reasons why I would enjoy visiting (city).

■ Three reasons why the city of ____ is an important cultural or exciting center in (country).

■ When cities build museums and other attractions, they can expect at least three important results.

■ There are at least three causes for the growth (or decline) of a city.

■ A Memorable Day in (city). (Use information on physical features as well as other information).

■ Three historic places you should visit in (city). (Select from physical features, major attractions, and major industries).

In addition, students could do any of the following activities:

■ Design a travel brochure
■ Make a poster
■ Create a street map
■ Create a public transportation map
■ Make an annotated list of major attractions: museums, parks, public buildings
■ Make a Who's Who book of famous people from a particular city

When teaching continents, teachers may wish to divide their students into groups and have each group research a particular aspect of the continent. Continents are both natural and political divisions, and in today's global world, students from at least fourth grade on through high

River Profile

Select a city and its river that you would like to know more about. Draw a map showing the path or flow of the river and indicate where the cities are along that river. Then tell how the city you chose benefits from the river it is on.

Name of River _____

Country/Countries Where It Flows _____

Continent/Continents Where It Flows _____

Length of River _____ miles

_____ kilometers

Source of River _____

Mouth of River _____

Special Features (e.g., waterfalls, rapids, reservoirs, dams) _____

_____

Major Cities along River _____

_____

Major Bridges That Cross River _____

_____

Other Information _____

_____

Figure 9.4

City Profile

Select a city that interests you or you would like to visit and complete the Profile. Then create a project that would interest other students about this city.

Name of City _____

State (if in a country with states) or Province (if in a country with provinces)

_____

Country in Which City Is Located _____

Area of City _____

Population _____

Waterways, Mountains, or Other Physical Features

_____

Major Attractions: 1) _____

2) _____

3) _____

4) _____

5) _____

Major Industries

_____

City Motto (if any) _____

City Nickname (if any) _____

Description of City Flag _____

People of Accomplishment from this City

_____

Other Information _____

Figure 9.5

school need to learn about these aspects of continents. Following are suggested areas of study:

- Rivers and other waterways
- Mountains and other land divisions
- Natural disasters (e.g., floods, hurricanes, earthquakes, volcanic eruptions)

Continent Profile

Select a continent that you would like to know more about and complete the profile. Create an interesting project and incorporate essential written information.

Name of Continent _____

Waterways Surrounding Continent _____

_____

Land Divisions Separating Continent from Other Continent (e.g., mountain) _____

_____

Area of Continent_____

Population _____

Three to Five Countries on Continent (except for Australia)

_____

_____

Major River or Rivers _____

_____

Mountains or Mountain Chains _____

_____

_____

Three to Five Natural Resources _____

_____

Significant or Unusual Animal Life _____

_____

Other Information _____

_____

Figure 9.6

- Countries within the continent
- Indigenous people and ethnic groups
- Railroads and other transportation systems continent-wide
- Explorers, conquerors, and early settlers associated with the continent

Students also can

- Design posters
- Create travel brochures
- Create various maps—physical, product, resource, language, climate
- Write to the World Health Organization at the United Nations for information on health, population, and food consumption

Combining Who's Who and Where in the World

The strategy Who's Who combines naturally with Where in the World, especially in the study of explorers and explorations. It is probably through such study that students today learn whatever geography they know. In his delightful and informative books *Don't Know Much About Geography* (1994) and *Don't Know Much About History* (1995), Kenneth C. Davis provides thumbnail sketches about explorers of the world that should fascinate students who are interested in adventure and discovery. Teachers can use a Taxonomy of these explorers and an Explorer Profile for enticing their students to find out about these people and write summary biographies or create books of explorers organized either chronologically or alphabetically (from A to V, if not to Z).

TAXONOMY SHEET

Worldwide Explorers

Trace the voyages of any of the following explorers. Include the country the explorer sailed from and the places in the world he uncovered or touched upon. Use a map to show the routes.

A	Amundsen
B	Balboa, Bellinghausen, Bering, Bingham, Bougainville, Bridger, Burton
C	Columbus, Cortes, Coronado, Cartier, Cook, Cabot, Champlain, Clark, Cousteau
D	DaGama, Drake, DeLeon, Dias, Darwin
E	Eric the Red, Ericson
F	Frobisher, Fremont
G	Gray
H	Hawkins, Henson, Hillary
I	
J	Joliet
K	Marquette
L	LaSalle, Lewis, Livingston
M	Magellan, Mackenzie, Mallory
N	
O	Orellana
P	Polo, Pizzaro, Perry, Powell
Q	
R	Ricci, Raleigh, Ross
S	Selkirk, Scott, Speke, Stanley, Schleimann
T	
U	
V	Vespucci, Verrazzano, Vancouver
W	
X	
Y	
Z	

Figure 9.7

Explorer Profile

Select an explorer who interests you and complete the following profile. Then, use a map to trace the explorations of that explorer. Write a summary statement that tells three to five contributions this explorer made to our geographic knowledge.

Name of Explorer _____

Years of Explorer's Life _____

_____

Nationality of Explorer _____

_____

Major Places of Exploration

_____

_____

Major Contributions to Geographic Knowledge

_____

_____

_____

_____

_____

Other Information _____

_____

_____

_____

Figure 9.8

TAXONOMY SHEET
Geographer's Companions

Below is a list of various occupations associated with geography. Select three or four of these occupations and use Defining Format or Career Profile to describe them. Then try to locate a person in one of these occupations and write a letter asking that person to tell you something about her or his work.

A	archaeologist, astronomer, agriculturist, agronomist, anthropologist
B	botanist
C	cartographer, climatologist
D	demographer
E	economist, explorer
F	financier
G	geologist, geometrician
H	horticulturist
I	
J	journalist
K	
L	
M	meteorologist, mathematician, mountain climber
N	navigator
O	oceanographer
P	political scientist
Q	
R	
S	seismologist, sociologist
T	
U	
V	
W	
X	
Y	
Z	zoologist, zoographer

Figure 9.9

Integrating Where in the World Across the Curriculum

While social studies teachers assume they are including geography in their curriculum, teachers of other subjects, such as science, mathematics, and foreign languages, may not always see the connection or may feel they do not have the time (or interest) to relate their subject to global issues or aspects. Teachers can use simple Taxonomies and writing suggestions that integrate geographical concepts with content area topics to show students the interrelationships of place to events, people, animals, and other subject matter.

Two useful Taxonomies are Geographer's Companions (see Figure 9.9) and Geographer's Measurements (see Figure 9.10). Geographer's Companions shows the careers requiring a knowledge of geography and also points out that someone who likes and studies geography has a wide choice of careers. These Taxonomies can be started by the teacher who suggests a few terms and continued by the students as they think of other terms or learn about them during their course of study. By focusing on careers, students discover that studying geography opens the door to exciting careers and jobs that may not be discussed in classrooms or career guidance sessions.

The Geographer's Measurements Taxonomy provides important geographic terms related to mathematics. Students select those terms appropriate to their needs and set up Defining Formats to explain their meanings. Students can use this Taxonomy to branch out into related topics.

For example, students can do historical research on the origins of Greenwich Mean Time or the International Date Line or use the terms to research careers (e.g., careers related to population include census taker, demographer, urban planner, cartographer, mathematician, etc.).

The English language as it is used today is both a polyglot language and a global language. In the words of Ralph Waldo Emerson, "The English language is the sea which receives tributaries from every region under heaven" (cited in *The Story of English*, McCrum, Cran and MacNeil 1986, 11). English also is the language that sends American tributaries to every region of the world. Yet, this wonderfully rich and diverse composition of the English language that has borrowed words from the world's languages and contributed its own words to other languages is seldom discussed in the classroom and is almost never mentioned during "traditional" grammar lessons. Only in the occasional social studies classroom does the teacher mention the extensive migrations of the Aryan people of India who gave the world the family of languages that later would be called Indo-European. And only a small number of students know the date 1066 and its significance in bringing into the English lexicon thousands of French words.

When teachers admonish students for using "ain't," they neglect to tell of its origin and reasons for its use and historic disapprobation. And they almost never point out to students why the "be" verb has been used in forms such as "I be here" compared to "I was here" or "I am here." All most students know is that some of these forms are incorrect.

TAXONOMY SHEET

Geographer's Measurements

Find the terms in the Taxonomy that represent measurement. Then check in your mathematics book or other resource to find the specific unit of measurement, or how much the terms equal, or how they are measured.

A	area, acre, arc
B	boundary
C	circumference, Celsius
D	degrees, density
E	equator, equinox, elevation
F	Fahrenheit
G	Greenwich Mean Time
H	Hemisphere
I	International Date Line
J	
K	kilometer
L	longitude, latitude
M	meter, meridian, mile
N	nadir
O	orbit
P	population
Q	
R	radiant
S	solstice, scale, sphere, syzygy
T	
U	
V	vector
W	
X	
Y	
Z	yard, zenith

Figure 9.10

Figures 9.11–9.14 shows several language-related Taxonomies and writing activities that will enhance students' understanding of the language they speak and its geographic connections.

TAXONOMY SHEET

Languages Around the World

This Taxonomy is a sampling of the languages of the world. Choose one language from the Taxonomy. Then research information about that language on the Internet or in an encyclopedia or other reference book. Complete the Language Profile and present the information to your classmates. (You may add other languages to this list.)

A	Albanian, Amharic, Afrikaans, Arabic, Armenian
B	Bulgarian, Bengali, Burmese
C	Czech, Chinese, Croatian
D	Dutch, Danish
E	English
F	Finnish, Farsi, French
G	German, Greek
H	Hungarian, Hebrew, Hindi
I	Icelandic, Italian
J	Japanese
K	Kirundi, Khmer, Korean
L	Lao
M	Malagasy, Mongolian
N	Norwegian, Nepali, Navajo
O	
P	Polish, Portuguese
Q	Quechua
R	Rumanian, Russian
S	Swedish, Serbian, Somali, Swahili
T	Turkish, Thai, Tagalog
U	Urdu, Ukraine
V	Vietnamese
W	
X	
Y	Yiddish
Z	Zuni

Figure 9.11

Language Profile

Name of Language

_____

Countries or Places Where Spoken

_____

Number of People Speaking this Language

_____

Family or Branch (e.g., Indo-European, Semitic, Native American)

_____

Writing System (e.g., Latin alphabet, Greek alphabet, Kanji characters)

Numbers from One to Ten

_____

_____

Five Other Words and Their English Meanings

1.

_____

2.

_____

3.

_____

4.

_____

5.

_____

Other Information

_____

_____

Figure 9.12

TAXONOMY SHEET

Je Parle Français (I Speak French)

In the year 1066, William of Normandy (a province that is now part of France) crossed the English Channel with his army and defeated Harold, the English ruler. England was now under the rule of a French-speaking government and would remain under Norman (French) rule for one hundred years. When the Normans were finally driven out of England, the English people were speaking a language that had added hundreds and hundreds of French words. This Taxonomy contains words that are used in English, but are of French origin. Find those that you don't know and look up their meanings in a college dictionary. Then write a story using as many French words as you can.

A	adieu, au revoir
B	boutique, bonbon, bon voyage, bouquet, bourgeois, ballet
C	chauffour, café, carte blanche, croissant, cachet
D	dejà-vu, dossier
E	esprit de corps, ennui
F	fête, fondue
G	gauche, genre, gratin
H	hospice, hors-d'oeuvre
I	imprimatur, ingenue
J	joie de vivre
K	kiosk
L	lingerie, legèrdemain, liqueur
M	madame, maître d', Mademoiselle, menu, massage
N	noblesse oblige, nouvelle cuisine
O	objet d'art, oblique, oui
P	petite, panorama, parachute, parasol, partisan, pièce de resistance, premier, protégé, promenade, potpourri
Q	quiche, queue
R	raison d'être, rapport, regime, rendezvous, RSVP
S	savoir-faire, sauté, soirée, souvenir, suite
T	tête-à-tête, tour de force, tout de suite
U	unique
V	valet, vaudeville, vestibule, vogue
W	
X	
Y	
Z	zeste

Figure 9.13

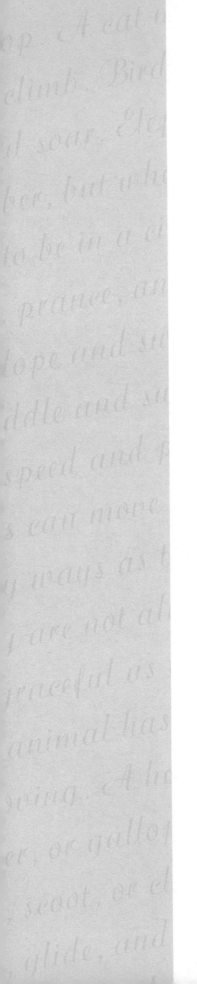

TAXONOMY SHEET

Hablo Español (I Speak Spanish)

The Spanish language, like English, is spoken in many parts of the world. You would speak Spanish in Spain, in most countries in South America, in Central America and Mexico, in Puerto Rico and the Dominican Republic, and in other places where Spanish-speaking people settled. Look up the meanings of the words on the Taxonomy that you don't know. Then write a story using as many of these Spanish words as you can. You can add other Spanish words to this list.

A	arroz, adobe, amigo
B	burrito
C	caballero, casa
D	dinero
E	enchilada
F	fiesta
G	gracias, gusto
H	hacienda, hasta la vista
I	
J	junta
K	
L	llama
M	muchacho, muchacha, maestro, mañana, mesa, mucho, momento, madre
N	
O	
P	patio, pollo, poncho, padre
Q	
R	ranchero, redondo
S	sombrero, serape, señorita, salsa
T	taco, tortilla, tío, tía
U	
V	
W	
X	
Y	
Z	zapatos

Figure 9.14

LINKING TO THE COMPUTER

For getting global information, the Internet is a window to the world. Internet users can find a person's street and e-mail address and maps of countries, states, cities, and local streets. They can click on an image of a country and link to sites that provide information about almost everything a person would want to know about that country. There are Web sites for countries, cities, languages, alphabets and other writing systems, people to contact, organizations providing free materials, and whatever else a student needs to "get acquainted" with the world beyond. With the vast up-to-date, quick accessibility of information on the Internet and through the use of encyclopedias available as CD-ROMs, students can access a wide array of material quickly and can thus take better advantage of it than they would be able to with traditional print materials. Yet, as teachers have already discovered, this behemoth of information must be used carefully and wisely. Students may not know how to go about getting the information they want. They, like many adults, can be easily distracted by the numerous links that move them away from their goals or purposes. More significant is the temptation to download material and submit another person's work as one's own because it seems a waste of time to rewrite it in one's own words. By suggesting which strategies to use— Taxonomies, Defining Format, Biographic Format, or others—teachers can help students stay focused and provide tools to help organize the myriad information available through CD-ROM resources and the Internet.

CHAPTER 10

Premises, Premises

The Book, the Play, the Movie

But will it make a good movie?

—Samuel Goldwyn

BETTERING THE BOOK REPORT

The book report has undoubtedly been the most used, overused, or even abused form of student writing from the beginning of American education to today. Who can't remember choosing a book with a book jacket to help "get started" on writing a report? Or reading a short book in order to write a short, easy report? Or wondering why they couldn't just read the book and enjoy it without having to tell "why I enjoyed this book"?

An alternative to the book report or a possible extension of book report writing is to have students plan making a movie from a book they have enjoyed reading. In creating a movie from a book, the students will be involved in a written genre that requires them to grasp the essence, also called the premise, of what the author is saying and convey this essence to an audience who may not have read the book. In addition, a good movie shows the interrelationship of the characters and depicts or highlights each character's traits, longings or needs, and growth or changes. In creating a movie from a biography, the filmmaker highlights the beliefs, accomplishments, behavior, and growth or journey of the biographical subject. As students change a book into a movie (either by imagination or in actual filming), they learn new and specialized vocabulary, explore human emotions such as loneliness and fear, learn about new places, and practice the writing forms of the world of films and movies. They realize from this activity that a book made into a movie recreates the joy and excitement that the book originally brought to the reader.

taxonomies

composing with
keywords

metacognition

defining format

profiles
and frames

who's who?

reasons, causes,
results

where in
the world

premises, premises

quotable quotes

personifications
and interactions

morphology,
etymology,
and grammar

PREMISES, PREMISES—THE BOOK AS A MOVIE

The development or planning of a movie generally begins with a premise, or the Premise Statement, a statement that succinctly states what the movie is about. Writing a Premise Statement requires the reader to have a clear understanding of the main or most significant character in the story, how the character interacts with other characters, how the character fits into the plot or action, and how the character grows, changes, or develops. All of this information must be stated (in the world of moviemaking) in no more than three paragraphs, oftentimes in just one paragraph. From the Premise Statement, the other aspects of the movie are developed: the treatment or fuller version of the story, the Character Profiles that describe the characters in detail, the storyboards that show the main scenes or sequence of the story, and the characters' dialogue.

By involving students in planning how to make a book into a movie, or possibly filming one or several scenes from a book, they become involved in the application of writing and have the opportunity to see their writing come alive. In addition, they are not only writing in the various genres of moviemaking (premise, treatment, dialogue) but are becoming familiar with the various roles or occupations of filmmaking or moviemaking.

Writing the Premise

In preparing students to plan a book as a movie, they first need to know how to write the Premise Statement, or Premise. The structure of the Premise has two parts: a statement about the main character, followed by the word *who* and a statement that tells the action or behavior of the main character that prompts the story or plot.

The Premise Statement can be thought of as a Frame (or framed sentence) with these components: The story _____ (name of story) by _____ (author) is about _____ (name of main character) who _____ (action or behavior of character related to plot).

For example, if the class were using *Charlotte's Web,* the first draft of the Premise would be as follows: The story *Charlotte's Web* by E. B. White is about a pig named Wilbur who is saved from being killed by his owner through the help of Charlotte, a spider, and other animals on the farm.

With the creation of the first draft of the Premise, the teacher guides the students into developing all of the other aspects of making a book into a movie, which include expansion of the Premise, building a Taxonomy of Filmmaking Terms, writing the treatment, and planning as many aspects of the movie as time, facilities, and equipment (camera, sets, costumes, etc.) allow.

Teaching the Premise Statement

Teachers can begin by telling students they will be reading (or hearing) a story that they will plan to make into a movie. As you introduce the idea, they can set up a Taxonomy or have the students develop their own pertaining to the vocabulary of filmmaking (a term generally used in contrast to moviemaking). The person who chooses the story from which the movie will be made (most likely the teacher) is called the *developer*—a term that should be included on the Taxonomy chart. If you have selected the story for a possible film, identify yourself as the developer and put this word on the Taxonomy chart. After the teacher and the students have heard or read the story, start the film preparation plan by teaching the class how to write the Premise. Define the Premise as a short statement about the story that is sent to a person called a *producer,* who is like a manager or organizer for making the movie. The Premise can be as short as a long sentence (as shown in the following example) or it can be three or four sentences. The purpose of the Premise is to interest the producer in making the story into a movie. Add the words *producer* and *Premise* to the Taxonomy.

Write the following Frame on the chalkboard or overhead:

The story _____ by
_____ is about
_____ who
_____.

For example, if the class were using *The Tale of Peter Rabbit* by Beatrix Potter, the first draft of the Premise could be as follows:

> The story The Tale of Peter Rabbit by Beatrix Potter is about a rabbit named Peter who steals vegetables from Mr. McGregor's garden and gets into trouble.

Then guide the students to revise and expand upon the Premise. Prompt the students to add details that a producer would need to know in considering the cast, the setting, and the plot of this story. Following is an example of a teacher-guided, revised, and expanded Premise.

> The story The Tale of Peter Rabbit by Beatrix Potter is about Peter, the youngest of four rabbits, living with his mother and siblings near a cabbage

patch, who does not pay attention to his mother's warnings about danger and sneaks into grouchy Mr. McGregor's garden to eat Mr. McGregor's delicious vegetables.

Character Profile

Name of Character

_____

Age _____

Family

_____

_____

Habitat

_____

_____

Wishes

_____

_____

_____

Fears

_____

_____

_____

Character Traits

_____

_____

Other Information

_____

_____

Figure 10.1

The Premise now has details of age, family, and location, followed by the word *who* and a statement that gives additional details about the action or behavior of the main character that prompts the story or plot. After students have practiced the Premise format several times, they will be able to construct their own Premise Statements independently.

The next writing task is to guide the students in developing Character Profiles. In *Playmaking*, Daniel Judah Sklar (1991) provides a step-by-step approach for students writing and performing their own plays. One student will need to be the *casting agent*, a person who knows the details about each character in order to choose the actors for the movie. (Add *casting agent* to the Taxonomy.)

Figure 10.1 is a Character Profile that can be used for characters in any book, movie, or play. Figures 10.2 and 10.3 are completed Profiles that represent the two opposing characters in Beatrix Potter's story and that were created in response to an assignment to focus in detail on each character and to think deeply and inferentially for nonexplicit information. Students will need to infer certain information, such as the rabbits' ages, which oftentimes will be representative of the reader's own age or personal characteristics.

Character Profile

Name of Character   Peter Rabbit

Age   four years old

Family   Mother, Flopsy (5 years old), Mopsy (6 years old), Cotton-tail (7 years old)

Father has died in an accident

Habitat   a sandbank under the root of a very big fir tree

Wishes   to eat Mr. McGregor's delicious vegetables

to do things by himself without his sisters and brother

Fears   to get caught by Mr. McGregor

to be put into a pie by Mrs. McGregor

to be punished by his mother

Character Traits   mischievous, disobedient

Other Information   he cries when he gets caught, he doesn't like to take his medicine

Flopsy, Mopsy, and Cotton-tail listen to their mother

Figure 10.2

Character Profile

Name of Character   Mr. McGregor

Age   38

Family   his wife Mrs. McGregor and three children—Mary 10, Molly 12, Max 14

Habitat   small farmhouse with a vegetable garden for lettuce, French beans, radishes, cabbage, and parsley

Wishes   to keep rabbits out of his garden so that his vegetables can grow

to have enough food for his wife and children

Fears   that his vegetables would be spoiled by rabbits

Character Traits   angry, sometimes mean to rabbits

kind to his to wife and children

Other Information

_____

_____

_____

Figure 10.3

From these two Character Profiles, the students will be able to recognize point of view. They can see that Mr. McGregor is not totally mean or unreasonable in defending his garden. Peter, on the other hand, is mischievous and disobedient but fortunately has a strict, caring mother. When the students are ready to write the script and play act the story, they will have a deeper understanding of the characters. Students also can complete Character Profiles on the other characters—the mother and the siblings—in preparation for casting.

Writing the Treatment

The treatment is the complete story retold simply for the preparation of the storyboard and script. The treatment also provides the student with the opportunity to recapitulate the story, making sure that the necessary details are included. Here is the partial continuation of the Peter Rabbit story from the Premise as dictated to the teacher by a group of first grade students at the end of the school year.

> Mrs. Rabbit had to go shopping to buy a brown bread and five buns. She told her children to stay close to the house and not go to Mr. McGregor's garden. Flopsy, Mopsy and Cotton-tail listened to her and only picked blackberries. But Peter didn't listen. He was a bad boy and sneaked into Mr. McGregor's garden. Then he ate so much vegetables that he got a stomach ache. Suddenly Mr. McGregor jumped out and ran after Peter with a rake in his hand. "Stop thief," he yelled. Peter was so scared. He ran so fast that he lost both of his shoes. Then he got trapped by a net and tore his buttons off his jacket. He started to cry and cry and cry.

Because writing the treatment can be a lengthy process even for older students, the class can be divided into groups of four and each group asked to write a portion of the story in sequence. In this way, the students get the practice of both retelling and sequencing.

Preparing the Storyboard

The storyboard is a sequence of scenes that represent the entire story. In essence, it is like a series of snapshots that when appropriately arranged tell an entire story. From the treatment, the students, preferably in groups, either write out the story by scenes or illustrate the scenes of the story. Young students generally want to illustrate the story, but older students may prefer words to pictures. The storyboard for *Peter Rabbit* may look something like that shown in Figure 10.4, which is a combination of students' sentences to which their illustrations would be added.

In the primary grades, students may improvise the lines of the story rather than memorize them. By having a narrator read the scene statements (as in the Storyboard shown in figure 10.4), the students playing the parts will most likely have memorized what each person has said, which is in effect an improvised script.

Storyboard for the Tale of Peter Rabbit by Beatrix Potter
Adapted by Mrs. Thomas's First Grade Class

Scene 1

Mrs. Rabbit talks to her children.

"You may go into the fields or down the lane, but don't go into Mr. McGregor's garden. Your father had an accident there and was put into a pie by Mrs. McGregor. I am going out, so don't get into mischief."

Scene 2

Peter sneaks out of the house and runs to Mr. McGregor's garden.

"I just love eating these vegetables. Lettuce, French beans, radishes are so delicious. Oooh, I'm getting a stomach ache. Maybe I should eat some parsley."

Scene 3

Peter meets Mr. McGregor at the cabbage patch.

"Get out of my garden you thief. If I catch you, I'll tell my wife to put you in a pie, just like we did to your father. Stop thief! Stop! Stop!"

Scene 4

Peter runs out of the garden.

"Oh, I'm lost. I can't find the gate out. Oh, I just lost my shoe. There goes my other shoe. More trouble. Now I'm caught in a net with my buttons. I'll never get out. Help! Help!"

Scene 5

Peter is rescued by friendly sparrows.

"Don't cry Peter. Just keep pushing till you get out of the net. We'll help pull you out."

Scene 6

Mr. McGregor catches up to Peter.

"I'll get you yet, you thief. I'll put this sieve over your head and you'll never get away now."

Continue the story in scenes 7 through 12

Figure 10.4

TAXONOMY SHEET

Set Design Places and Objects for The Tale of Peter Rabbit

A	
B	bed, basket, bread, buns, blackberries, beans, black currant bushes, blackberries, bowl
C	cups, cover, cucumber frame, cabbage, chamomile tea
D	
E	
F	French beans, flower pots
G	gate, garden
H	hoe
I	
J	
K	
L	lettuce, leaves
M	milk
N	netting
O	onions
P	pillow, parsley, potatoes, peas, pitcher
Q	
R	radishes, rake, rabbit hole
S	spoon, shovel, sieve
T	tree, tool shed, tablespoon
U	umbrella
V	
W	watering can, wheelbarrow
X	
Y	
Z	

Figure 10.5

SET DESIGN

Designing the set is not only fun for the students but provides them with the opportunity to learn about interior and exterior places and the items and objects that are part of the story. When students design or build sets, they have to focus on details. Appoint two or three students to work together as *set designers*. It will be their job to go through the book and list all the places and items either mentioned by the author or illustrated by the artist. After they have compiled the list, they present it to the class, who may then create the set. If the teacher wishes, she or he can have the whole class help the set designers. The set can be a simple mural or even a set of drawings that contain whatever objects can be gathered or even imagined. Most important is that the students are aware of the places and objects. For a Peter Rabbit production, the set designers made the list shown as Figure 10.5.

COSTUME DESIGN

Most students love to dress up in costumes. When acting out a story from an illustrated book, students can use the actual book to get ideas for costumes. Students or a student group can collect clothing items that can actually be used. But the learning aspect of this activity is getting the students to research what they need and making a plan for getting the items. In the Peter Rabbit story, the costume designers, with the help of the class, will have to look at the pictures in the book carefully and name what each cast member needs. They can use an organizational chart (see figure 10.6) to record information about the costumes.

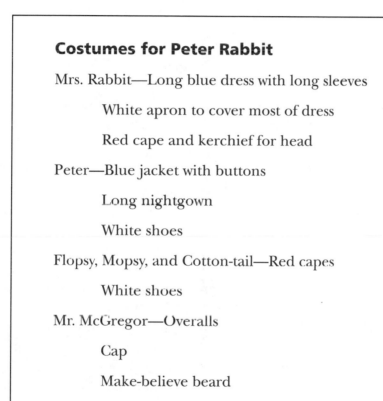

Costumes for Peter Rabbit

Mrs. Rabbit—Long blue dress with long sleeves

     White apron to cover most of dress

     Red cape and kerchief for head

Peter—Blue jacket with buttons

     Long nightgown

     White shoes

Flopsy, Mopsy, and Cotton-tail—Red capes

     White shoes

Mr. McGregor—Overalls

     Cap

     Make-believe beard

Figure 10.6

The Program and the Credits

Designing and writing the program is both a small group and class activity that involves the students in the publishing aspect of writing. They have to decide on a name for the film or presentation and a name for the company that has made the film. They also have to decide who will be actors, who will be production crew members, and who will create the set, the costumes, etc.

Credits for the Production of Peter Rabbit

The _____ Production

Company of Class _____ Presents

Title _____

By (Author) _____

Adapted for Filming By (Students)

_____

Produced By

_____

Directed By

_____

Casting By

_____

Cast

Character Actor, etc.

Script Writers

_____

Set Designers

_____

Costume Designers

_____

Artists

_____

Lighting

_____

Music

_____

Special Effects

_____

(Others)

Figure 10.7

The teacher can bring in sample programs from plays, musicals, or other presentations to show students the elements to be included and the design and layout features. Students also can watch a movie on video and read the credits, noting who is listed, how names are presented, and other relevant information. People who love movies always watch the credits and realize how many professionals are involved in making a film. Figure 10.7 provides a template of a program from a second grade class that had presented _Peter Rabbit_ and also filmed it.

By the completion of the production, the students will have finished the Taxonomy on Filmmaking (or Moviemaking). Depending on time and interest, teachers can ask students to write a one-sentence statement of what the terms mean. For example, a producer is the person who organizes and manages the entire production of a movie. The Taxonomy should have the terms listed in Figure 10.8, plus any others the students come up with during this activity.

Book-to-Movie in the Intermediate Grades

For the middle grades for Book-to-Movie strategy, the emotionally stirring story _Number the Stars_ (1989) by Lois Lowry works particularly well. As soon as the students write the Premise of this book, they will immediately perceive its potential as a movie.

Number the Stars by Lois Lowry is about a ten-year-old Danish girl, Annemarie Johansen, living with her parents and younger sister Kirsti in Nazi-occupied Copenhagen (Denmark) during World War II (1940-1945) who has to help her family save her best friend Ellen Rosen and Ellen's family from being deported by the Nazis to a concentration camp along with other Jewish families.

With historical fiction, research teams can gather information about the historical background portrayed in a story. For example, students reading *Number the Stars* can form research teams to do the following:

- Complete a Country Profile on Denmark.
- Obtain information about the saving of the Danish Jews during World War II.
- Find out why Sweden was able and willing to admit Jews from Denmark.

By the intermediate grades, students can work in teams as scriptwriters, focusing on the dialogues of the different characters. Writing dialogue from a novel can be tricky because the students have to select or, at times, modify what the characters are saying in to order to keep the action moving. The students must also know that the screenwriter lets *the words speak for themselves* and gives very little, if any, narrative information. The example below was put together by two "screenwriters" in a fifth grade class reading *Number the Stars.*

> **Scene:** The kitchen of the Johansen house. Family is eating dinner. Curtains are drawn and only candles are burning at the table to give the family light.
>
> **Annemarie:** Is it true, Papa, that people say that all of Denmark is King Christian's bodyguard?
>
> **Papa:** Yes. It is true. Any Danish citizen would die for King Christian, to protect him.
>
> **Annemarie:** You too, Papa?
>
> **Papa:** Yes.

TAXONOMY SHEET

Filmmaking Taxonomy

The terms in this Taxonomy come from the world of filmmaking and playwriting. Add others you know to this list.

A	audience, actors, artists, author
B	book
C	character, costumes, casting agent, camera technician, credits
D	dialogue, developer, director
E	editor
F	fadeout
G	
H	
I	
J	
K	
L	lighting
M	music
N	
O	outline
P	premise, problem, producer
Q	
R	
S	scenes, setting, storyboard, set designer, special effects, scriptwriter
T	treatment
U	
V	
W	
X	
Y	
Z	

Figure 10.8

Annemarie: And Mama?

Papa: Mama too.

Annemarie: Then I would too, Papa, if I had to.

A brief silence as Mama takes away the dishes.

Annemarie: Sometimes I wonder why the king wasn't able to protect us. Why didn't he fight the Nazis so that they wouldn't come into Denmark with their guns?

Papa: We are such a tiny country. And they are such an enormous enemy. Our king was very wise. He knew how few soldiers Denmark had. He knew that many, many Danish people would die if we fought.

As suggested for the primary grades, students should create a Taxonomy for themselves to keep track of the terms they are using in moving from the Premise to the creation of the movie.

The Fairy Tale—A Book-to-Movie Activity for Intermediate and Middle School Students

The traditional fairy tales—meaning those recorded by Jacob and Wilhelm Grimm (in German), Charles Perrault (in French), and Joseph Jacobs (in English)—have been the cultural glue of Western literature. In his insightful work *The Uses of Enchantment,* psychologist Bruno Bettelheim points out that the fairy tales

> The fairy tale simplifies all situations. Its figures are clearly drawn; and details, unless very important, are eliminated. All characters are typical rather than unique (Bettelheim 1975, 8).

Because of these characteristics, fairy tales

> came to convey . . . overt and covert meanings—came to speak simultaneously to all levels of the human personality, communicating in a manner which reaches the uneducated mind of the child as well as that of the sophisticated adult (Bettelheim 1975, 5).

From this point of view, Bettelheim promotes the absolute necessity of students knowing fairy tales for their powerful messages:

> . . . that a struggle against severe difficulties in life is unavoidable, is an intrinsic part of human existence—but that if one does not shy away, but steadfastly meets the unexpected and often unjust hardships, one masters all obstacles and at the end emerges victorious (Bettelheim 1975, 8).

Bettelheim's description of fairy tales moves them beyond the realm of stories for young children. When students in the intermediate and middle school grades are reintroduced to fairy tales, they perceive (usually for the first time) the messages of struggle, hardship, and the overcoming of obstacles that Bettelheim writes about. Goldilocks, Little Red Riding Hood, Snow White, and Cinderella each represent a different stage of growth or development, facing different situations that place them in danger or difficulty. These characters have adversaries and make mistakes or face challenges. These perspectives, detailed so brilliantly by Bettelheim, are captured in the following activities, which lend themselves to dramatization and filmmaking.

The Fairy Tale Genre

Begin by defining the elements of a fairy tale. A fairy tale is a special genre that usually has the following ingredients:

- Central character who usually (but not always) is female and not yet an adult, and who is faced with a difficult problem or dilemma.

- One or more characters who cause or add to the central character's problem.

- One or more characters who come to the aid of the central character.

- A way for the character to solve the problem or have the problem solved either through resourcefulness or with the help of others and a touch of magic.

Example—Snow White

Central character: Snow White, about 14 years old, growing up in a castle with only her stepmother.

Problem or dilemma: Stepmother becomes jealous as Snow White becomes more beautiful and decides to have Snow White killed.

Additional characters who add to the problem: A hunter is ordered by the stepmother to kill Snow White in the forest and bring proof of her death.

Additional characters who help the central character: Animals in the forest help Snow White find shelter in the house of the Seven Dwarfs, who try to protect Snow White from the pursuit of the stepmother.

Resolution or Solving of the Problem: Stepmother tempts Snow White with a comb, a girdle, and finally a beautiful but poisoned apple that causes Snow White to appear dead. Dwarfs keep her in a glass coffin; Prince arrives and through a kiss (the magic of love) revives Snow White.

WRITING A TREATMENT FOR FAIRY TALES

After the teacher and students have discussed and defined the elements found in most fairy tales, students then select a fairy tale and write a treatment that covers the three aspects of the story: the characters, the problem or dilemma, and the solution. The students can also add a personal reaction. By using this format, students will have expanded the Premise Statement into an original retelling that is preparatory to developing a storyboard and dialogue for Book-to-Movie presentation. Following is an example of a treatment written by a fifth grade student.

The Characters

Beauty and the Beast by Charles Perrault is about Beauty, an eighteen-year old young woman WHO asks her father to bring back just one rose from his trip to a faraway place. In addition, there are Beauty's two sisters WHO are greedy and want their father to bring back dresses and jewels and get angry at Beauty because they think she is just being too good by just asking for a rose. Then there is the father WHO wants to please all his daughters because he is a good father. After that comes a very important character, the Beast WHO once was a handsome prince but had a spell put on him by a wicked witch and is now very ugly.

The Problem

The problem in this story is that the father gets caught in a storm and lands by mistake at the Beast's house. The Beast gives the father food and a place to sleep, but in the morning the father steals a rose from the Beast's garden to bring back to Beauty. Now the Beast is very angry and tells the father that the only way he can go home to his family is if he sends his daughter Beauty to take his place. The father promises to do this, although he thinks in his mind that once he escapes he will not send Beauty. But when he gets home and gives Beauty the rose and tells her what happened, she says she must keep the promise her father made. So Beauty magically gets to the Beast's castle, but even though the Beast is kind to her, she is afraid of him because he is really very, very ugly. Beauty is now very sad, but she doesn't know what to do to solve her problem. Beauty gets so sad that the Beast feels sorry for her and tells her that she can go home for a short while to visit her father and her sisters. But he makes her promise that she will return in a few days. Beauty thanks the Beast for being so kind and magically gets home. Her father is very happy to see her, but her sisters still think she is acting too good and won't talk to her. Beauty doesn't want to leave her father, but then she has a dream that the Beast is dying because she didn't go back as she promised.

Solution to the Problem

The problem begins to be solved when Beauty tells her father that she has to go back to the Beast or else he will die. She magically gets back, but it is almost too late. The Beast is lying on the ground and can hardly breathe. When Beauty sees him she realizes that he has been very good to her and loves her. She also now loves him even though he is very ugly. But she doesn't care that he is ugly so she begs him to live and says, "I love you because you have been so good to me." When the Beast hears these words, he sits up and suddenly his ugly looks begin to change, first his hair, then his eyes, then his skin. Beauty is amazed. The Beast has suddenly become handsome. He then tells her, "A wicked witch turned me into a Beast and said only if someone really, truly loved me could I be changed back to a Prince." So Beauty and the Beast who was now a Prince got married and lived happily ever after.

My Reaction to the Story

As a result of reading Charles Perrault's story Beauty and the Beast, I now realize that we should love someone because they are good and kind, not just because they are handsome. I would recommend this story to everyone who believes this idea and needs to learn about this idea. This is truly my favorite fairy tale.

INNOVATING ON FAIRY TALES FOR DRAMATIC OR FILMED PERFORMANCES: PLAINTIFF *v* DEFENDANT

By using selected fairy tales, students can write from the point of view, or perspective, of one of the characters as if the characters were going to address the problem in a court of law. One character is the plaintiff, the other the defendant. Students write from the perspective of one character and tell the story from that character's point of view. The students also can write as an attorney for the defendant, attorney for the plaintiff, a witness for either side, or the judge.

Students can work in cooperative groups, each student writing from a different point of view, so that all of the characters are represented. When the writing is finished, the group can conduct a trial and the rest of the class can serve as the jury.

Following are familiar fairy tales and the problems in each that could be used in a Plaintiff *v.* Defendant assignment:

Goldilocks: Mrs. Bear sues Goldilocks' mother for the crime of irresponsibility and negligence in letting her daughter break in and enter the Bears' house.

Little Red Riding Hood: *Grandmother charges the wolf with physical harassment and intent to kill.*

Cinderella: *Cinderella charges her stepmother with abuse and negligence for making her work long hours at hard labor.*

Jack and the Beanstalk: *Giant sues Jack for break-in and theft, demanding recovery of stolen items.*

Before the students begin work on the "trial" they will need to work as a group to complete Character Profiles of the characters they are writing about. Provide each group with a Character Profile and explain each section as outlined below.

Age of Character: In many stories the age of the character is unspecified and the reader has to infer the age from the behavior. For example, the reader might infer that Little Red Riding Hood is about six or seven years old. This could be why she is unable to recognize that the wolf is the stranger her mother has warned her about. She naively tells the wolf where she is going. She is easily fooled by outward appearances when the wolf is dressed as her grandmother, and she is dependent upon being rescued by an adult (the woodcutter). Of course, these ideas are mature for young children, but through discussion and questioning, the students often reach a consensus on age.

Family: Here, too, there is inference. Again, in *Little Red Riding Hood,* no family members other than the mother and the grandmother are stated. However, the reader of the story might wonder if there are younger children in the household that necessitate the mother to send the oldest child on an errand alone. Students might wonder if the father is away or at work. Therefore, in completing this line, students might add other family members.

Habitat: The habitat should be described with as many details as possible. For example, Little Red Riding Hood lives in a three-room cottage at the northern end of a huge pine tree forest.

Wishes and Fears: Through discussion, the students begin to expand their ideas of the character's wishes and fears. Little Red Riding Hood is likely to wish that 1) her grandmother gets well, 2) she recognizes a stranger, 3) she doesn't have to go alone through the forest, 4) her mother would go instead, and so on. Similarly, the students have to consider all the fears of a young child making this trip alone.

Character Traits: The students need to be able to distinguish between behavioral traits and appearance traits. Bravery is a character trait, whereas beauty is an appearance trait. In addition, the students have to consider both positive and negative traits (generous versus selfish).

Preparation for Trial

Your group will be preparing a trial for one of the characters in a fairy tale that your group has selected. Complete the following information before the trial begins.

Name of Case _____

Plaintiff _____

Defendant _____

Attorney for the Plaintiff

_____

Attorney for the Defendant

_____

Witness(es) for the Plaintiff

_____

Witness(es) for the Defendant

_____

Plea of Defendant (Guilty or Not Guilty)

_____

Date of Trial _____

Location of Trial _____

Presiding Judge _____

Other Information

_____

_____

_____

Figure 10.9

Presenting Your Case

Choose who you will be in the trial: the plaintiff, the defendant, the attorney for the plaintiff, the attorney for the defendant, or a witness. Before you make your choice, read what role each of these people plays in a trial.

Your Name _____

Role in this Case _____

Write your presentation giving your side of the story with as much detail and credibility as possible.

- If you are the plaintiff, give specific accusations, citing at least three details that support your argument.
- If you are the defendant, give strong reasons why the charges against you are wrong or improbable.
- As a attorney for the plaintiff, you must make the strongest possible case against the defendant, providing numerous details of wrongdoing.
- As the attorney for the defendant, you must convince the jury that under no circumstances could your client have done the crime she or he is accused of.
- If you are a witness, you must establish that you are truthful, careful in what you say, and perfectly clear about what you have witnessed.

In your writing, first identify who you are:

> e.g., My name is Cunning B. Fox, and I am a witness for Hermit T. Wolf.

Explain your position by giving three significant arguments for or against the accusation. Give time and dates and very specific reasons for your actions or beliefs.

> e.g., I married Cinderella's father ten years ago when the little girl was barely five years old. I have always loved Cinderella and treated her as my own daughter.

Use positive words to describe yourself or your client.

> e.g., I'm a gentle giant, living my life on a mountaintop, bothering no one, caring for my lovely wife. All I have are a few simple possessions.

Figure 10.10

Below is a sampling of writing from sixth graders in a rural Tennessee school who wrote and videotaped the complete trial of *Sarah Hood v. Harry T. Wolf.*

Sarah Hood vs. Harry T. Wolf

Opening Argument Presented by T. J. Nakita, Attorney for Harry T. Wolf, Defendant

Ladies and gentlemen of the jury. I will prove that my client is in no way guilty of the alleged crime. First off, he is a Buddhist, and therefore a vegetarian. He respects and loves all living creatures and would die at the thought of eating any sort of meat. He wouldn't hurt a fly on the basis of his beliefs. He also has very bad stomach problems. You might call it an ulcer, so there is no way he could have eaten an entire woman and/or her granddaughter. I submit two pieces of evidence for the record, #310, his birth certificate, and #311, his doctor's statement.

Mr. Harry T. Wolf is indeed Buddhist as stated on his birth certificate and signed below by a Buddhist monk.

Tie Coug   *Tibetan Monk*

Harry T. Wolf   *Defendant*

Mr. Harry T. Wolf does indeed have an ulcer. Medical records of this condition are at the Central City Hospital.

Dr. Zeke Rathbun   *Chief of Stomach Problems*

Testimony of the Defendant Harry T. Wolf

Nakita: Mr. Wolf, please share your side of the story.

Mr. Wolf: I was sitting behind a tree eating a very full dinner, when I heard footsteps. I looked around and saw Little Red Riding Hood coming my way. I asked her where she was going and she said to her grandmother's house. I decided to be a nice gentleman by offering a short cut. After a while, I decided to see if she had made it there safely. She wasn't there yet and so I decided to wait for her inside. I was very tired from the walk and I saw some nightclothes. I decided to put them on and take a nap. I heard a scream from the kitchen. It was Grandmother Hood, so I put her in the closet just to get her quiet. Little Red then came in and so as not to scare her, I pretended to be Grandmother Hood. She gave me the goodies, and we talked for a while. When she left, I went to the closet to get the old Mrs. Hood. She was asleep, so I put her on the bed and left.

Book-to-Movie in the High School

In the high school, where short class modules and departmental schedules curtail dramatization of a book, students can use a modified version of the procedures in Book-to-Movie but still keep the elements of dramatization.

First, have the students write a Premise so they have a statement of what the book is about. Often, the Premise Statement can lead to a discussion as to why the book might or might not be a good movie. Who would be the audience for a movie with this premise? Would it have enough action or emotion? Have there been other successful movies with a similar premise? The teacher might want to have a class work in groups, with each group writing one treatment on a book the group has selected. Another aspect of the writing should be a Character Profile for understanding of the characters. Students reading *The Pigman* by Paul Zindel (1968), can work in groups of four or five, with each group responsible for completing a Character Profile of a different character. Then, the students in each group work together to keep a journal of the ongoing events in their character's life. After the journals have been completed, "actors" from each group play characters by taking turns reading from their journals so that the audience hears the different "voice" and point of view of each character.

Figure 10.11 shows a journal assignment based on *The Pigman* with sample entries written from the point of view of Mr. Pignati.

The concept of Premises, Premises is to provide students with a set of writing strategies related to making a book into a movie. Whether the students only plan the movie or actually make a film or video, they will have to practice a wide range of genres and develop skills in summary writing, retelling, sequencing and narrating, dialogue writing, character analysis, plus related skills of moviemaking such as research for set design, costume design, and historic authenticity. Premises, Premises will provide students with a repertory of writing activities that they will find lively, creative, and personally satisfying.

LINKING TO THE COMPUTER

As students become more proficient in using word processing programs, they can use the computer more often to compose their writing. Premises, Premises lends itself to using the computer to draft and refine scripts, monologues and dialogues, all of which are normally "typed" for both easy reading and aesthetics. Students also can use computers to create

Keeping a Journal

Imagine that you are one of the three main characters in *The Pigman*—John, Lorraine, or Mr. Pignati. Keep a journal of your interactions with the other two characters who affect your life. Write the journal from your point of view. Focus on your feelings and the changes that are taking place in your life. Use the outline of the story as a guide for your journal.

Chapter 4—The first contact by telephone between Mr. Pignati and Lorraine and John.

Example of Journal Entry by Angelo Pignati

This afternoon I got a call from a delightful young woman calling on behalf of a charity called the L & J Fund. Her name was Ms. Truman. She was not only friendly, but full of good jokes. I couldn't help laughing and then I told her about how my wife always laughs at my jokes. I told her the joke about the best get-well cards—four aces—and she laughed. Of course I said I would make a contribution to her cause. Such a nice young woman. She just brightened up my day.

Chapter 5—The first meeting of Mr. Pignati with Lorraine and John. Include the contribution and the pigs.

Chapter 6—The visit to the zoo.

Chapter 7—Mr. Pignati's wife.

Chapter 8—The visit to Beekman's Department Store

Chapter 10—Visiting Mr. Pignati; confessions and games

Chapter 11—Heart attack

Chapter 13—The party

Chapter 14—Apologies and death. Final entries and reflections

Figure 10.11

programs for their plays. In addition, students can use the Internet to search for and read synopses and reviews of movies as background for writing their own Premises and opinions.

Quotable Quotes

Beliefs and Opinions

To the uneducated, an A is just three sticks.

—A. A. Milne

QUOTABLE QUOTES—FOR REMEMBRANCE AND RESPONSE

Books are the human invention that contain the beliefs, opinions, and wisdom of those whose words have been captured and put into print. From these recorded words, authors often are inspired to add their own words. Quotable Quotes is the strategy that asks or inspires students to respond to specific quotations from literary characters or people of note or accomplishment. By having students read and ponder the words of others, they can respond with their own ideas and can be invited to respond with their own newly minted widsom of personal sayings, quotations, and maxims. In the strategy Quotable Quotes, the teacher points out or makes the students aware of statements or sayings that can inspire or be controversial and asks the students to write a personal response. An example is "Write your own response to Patrick Henry's words, 'Give me liberty or give me death.'" Teachers can provide specific Quotable Quotes and/or ask students to select their own Quotable Quotes from books, stories, newspaper articles, speeches, and other sources.

USING QUOTABLE QUOTES

The purpose of Quotable Quotes is to have students establish an imaginary dialogue with the characters or people who have made noteworthy

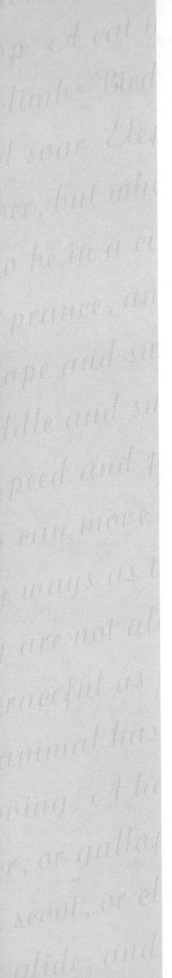

statements. In this dialogue, students express their own opinions or beliefs in relationship to the quoted statement, or Quotable Quote.

Students can be introduced to Quotable Quotes with quotes from nursery rhymes that can be used with primary grade student well into third grade, as well as with wonderful statements taken from classic children's and appropriate adult literature. Older students also can use Quotable Quotes for writing activities inspired by novels as well as the words of presidents, social activists, scientists, writers, and anyone else who has uttered words worth remembering.

Quotable Quotes from the World of Mother Goose

Many nursery rhymes are pithy stories written in rhyme that teach lessons or tell of human behaviors both positive and negative. Some rhymes tell of kindness, loyalty, hospitality, and industriousness; others tell of lateness, disobedience, or indifference to others. This wide range of behaviors, stated in charming, easy-to-memorize rhymes, can be the basis of class discussion, which can be followed by having students write their own ideas and beliefs. The writing can be in the form of letters to nursery rhyme characters expressing opinions or giving advice. Or students can respond in personal essays (Three Reasons Why) or journal entries in which they imagine themselves as a nursery rhyme character, such as Little Bo-Peep, going through the pain of losing one's sheep or other pet.

Since many nursery rhymes relate to values of kindness and gentleness, particularly to animals, they can serve as the stimulus for students to express their own feelings and values about similar topics. Following are examples of selected representative rhymes with suggestions for writing. Additional examples can be found in other poems and children's stories.

Kindness to Animals
After students hear these rhymes, they can write three ways in which they can be a good friend to animals or pets or write a letter to their favorite animal telling it how they can protect it.

> I like little kitty, her coat is so warm,
> And if I don't hurt her she'll do me no harm;
> So I'll not pull her tail, nor drive her away,
> But kitty and I very gently will play.
>
> The little robin grieves
> When the snow is on the ground.
> For the trees have no leaves,
> And no berries can be found.

SkyLight Professional Development

The air is cold, the worms are hid:
For robin here what can be done?
Let's strew around some crumbs of bread,
And then he'll live till snow is gone.

The north wind does blow
And we shall have snow,
And what will poor Robin do then?
Poor thing!
He'll sit in a barn
And keep himself warm,
And hide his head under his wing,
Poor thing!

Quotable Quotes from Children's Literature

The world of children's literature is filled with wise sayings, opinions, and beliefs expressed through human, animal, and other imagined characters. In *The Way Mothers Are,* a kitten worries if her mother still loves her even though she does "naughty things." The kitten gets various assurances from her mother but is not satisfied until her mother says, "So you think I love you just when you're good and stop loving you when you are naughty, do you? I love you all of the time, because you are mine" (Schlein 1966, unpaged). A quotation such as this can serve as the stimulus for many types of student writing, for example, Why I Love My [Mother, Father, Grandmother, etc.], How I Know My Mother Loves Me, and Why a Mother Animal Loves Its Baby.

In using children's literature, teachers can draw attention to Quotable Quotes by writing them on the chalkboard and bulletin boards. Teachers also can ask students to select their favorite Quotable Quotes and write them in their notebooks. Using Quotable Quotes as motivators and springboards for writing can be used continuously through the grades to help students not only read but to interact with the literary characters.

Among the many examples of children's stories with Quotable Quotes are A. A. Milne's classic stories of Winnie the Pooh and his friends, who reflect the concerns and thoughts of young children everywhere. Following are several quotes and questions that can be used as a springboard for discussion and writing.

From the Wisdom of Pooh Himself

> *For I am a Bear of Very Little Brain, and long words*
> *Bother me (Milne 1957, 50).*

Question: How do you feel about long words?

Question: Can you make a Taxonomy of your favorite long words?

> *My spelling is Wobbly. It's good spelling, but it Wobbles,*
> *and the letters get in the wrong places (Milne 1957, 78).*

Question: Why do you think the letters get in the wrong places?

Question: What advice would you give to Pooh about spelling?

From Piglet

> *It is awfully hard to be b-b-brave when you are only a*
> *Very Small Animal (Milne 1957, 89).*

Question: What can a small animal do to protect itself from bigger animals?

Quotable Quotes from *The Phantom Tollbooth* by Norton Juster

In a world of wonderful books for intermediate grade students, *The Phantom Tollbooth* by Norton Juster (1989) is an excellent book to read aloud and use for post-reading writing activities. This novel tells the story of Milo, a spoiled boy of about ten or eleven who is totally bored by his abundance of toys and gadgets, including his own car. Then one day he gets a tollbooth as a gift from his uncle and, taking his car through the tollbooth, he enters a land "beyond expectations." Milo's life will never be the same, and Milo's adventures and new understandings can be vicariously shared by students. Following are quotes from *The Phantom Tollbooth* that can be used to inspire reflection and discussion, as well as serve as prompts for writing.

From the character the Whether Man

> *Expectations is the place you must always go to before*
> *you get where you're going (Juster 1989, 19).*

Question: What are your expectations?

Question: What dreams do you have that are "beyond your expectations"?

From the Spelling Bee

> *Then one day I realized that I'd never amount to any-*
> *thing without an education and, being naturally adept*
> *at spelling, I decided that . . . (Juster 1989, 52).*

Question: You probably guessed that the Spelling Bee decided to become a champion speller. What are three good reasons for knowing how to spell correctly?

From Rhyme and Reason

> *Words and numbers are of equal value, for, in the cloak*
> *of knowledge, one is warp and the other woof (Juster*
> *1989, 77).*

Question: On a loom, the lengthwise threads are called the warp and the threads that are interwoven is the woof. How would our lives be different if suddenly numbers were to disappear?

From Alec, a boy who stands in mid-air and grows down instead of growing up

> *You can never hurt yourself falling down if you're in*
> *mid-air . . . (Juster 1989, 106).*

Question: What reasons would you give Alec for "growing up"?

From Reason, *one of the twins*

> *You often learn more by being wrong for the right reasons*
> *than you do by being right for the wrong reasons (Juster*
> *1989, 233).*

Question: Think of something you did that might have been a mistake. What did you learn from that mistake?

Quotable Quotes from Aesop, the Writer of Fables, and Other (Unknown) Moralists

Aesop, the moralist of antiquity, has given the world the pithy statements that come in handy when one wants to prove a point. Whether or not he wrote the stories for these numerous aphorisms, no one knows, but when most people think of fables, they most likely think of Aesop. Other authors of fables include Jean de la Fontaine, the French fabulist of the seventeenth century, who probably is best known for *The Fox and the Crow.*

Students generally enjoy writing fables because they contain characters that are simply drawn, a direct plot, and an ending that is known before the story starts.

Students may, at some time in their school years, be asked to rewrite a fable to fit the moral. A variant on such a writing exercise is to ask students to write the consequences of ignoring the moral or lesson, or to think about the contradiction in the lesson. Here are several Quotable Quotes from Aesop, with an added statement. Ask students to select two or three of these statements and write what happens or what a person should do when the moral or lesson is ignored.

- If too many cooks spoil the soup, describe the soup that too many cooks spoiled.
- If in unity there is strength, tell what happens when groups split apart.
- If slow and steady wins the race, tell what happens to those who speed and then dawdle.
- If we should make hay while the sun shines, what should we do on a rainy day?
- If silence is golden, why do we speak?
- If haste makes waste, when should we work slowly?

HISTORICAL QUOTABLE QUOTES

To many students, the study of history seems to be about dates and battles or the rise and fall of civilizations. Yet, history is about humans, most of whom are simply caught up in the march of events while others seem to make history happen. Most of the people who make history happen have made statements that get quoted, and often these people are remembered not only for what they did but for what they said. The following Quotable Quotes are from American presidents, fighters for freedom and equal rights, and women who have spoken out specifically for women's issues.

Quotable Quotes of American Presidents

All through the study of American history, students hear the words of many of the American presidents and may discuss their meaning or importance in social studies classrooms. Following are prompts for responding to the selection of Quotable Quotes of several American presidents. Students can use them as starters for their own ideas and opinions on the issue stated in the quote.

Select one of the quotations taken from the speech of an American president. Then write three paragraphs. In each paragraph, write a different reason to support the statement you selected.

> *I believe this country cannot endure permanently half slave and half free.*
> —ABRAHAM LINCOLN

> *Walk softly and carry a big stick.*
> —THEODORE ROOSEVELT

> *The only thing we have to fear is fear itself—nameless, unreasoning, unjustified terror which paralyzes needed efforts to convert retreat into advance.*
> —FRANKLIN D. ROOSEVELT

> *Ask not what your country can do for you, but what you can do for your country.*
> —JOHN F. KENNEDY

> *The Great Society is a place where every child can find knowledge to enrich his knowledge and to enlarge his talents.*
> —LYNDON B. JOHNSON

Quotable Quotes in the Fight for Freedom and Equal Rights

From the very beginning of American history, words have played a role in shaping individuals' ideas and actions. Throughout most people's schooling, students hear (if they are listening) the words of Patrick Henry, Benjamin Franklin, and Thomas Paine. As they move through the years, they consider the calls or messages of Davy Crockett, Chief Joseph, Earl Warren, and Martin Luther King, Jr. Following are several of these truly Quotable Quotes with suggestions for student reactions and responses. Teachers can add their own favorites as well as those offered by their students.

> *I know not what course others may take, but as for me give me liberty or give me death.*
> —PATRICK HENRY TO THE VIRGINIA HOUSE
> OF BURGESSES ON MARCH 20, 1755

Suggestion: Write your own definition of liberty. Then tell why liberty, as you defined it, is important to you.

> *These are the times that try men's souls.*
> —THOMAS PAINE IN HIS PAMPHLET
> "COMMON SENSE," WRITTEN AROUND 1775

Suggestion: Every period in history has its difficult times. Imagine that you are writing a letter to Thomas Paine and are using his quote to tell him that there are events today that "try men's souls." Tell him what two or three of those events are and why we are struggling over them.

> *We conclude that in the field of public education the doctrine of 'separate but equal' has no place.*
> —STATED BY CHIEF JUSTICE EARL WARREN IN
> THE UNANIMOUS OPINION OF THE SUPREME
> COURT IN THE CASE OF BROWN V. THE BOARD OF
> EDUCATION OF TOPEKA, MAY 17, 1954

Suggestion: After you have studied this significant Supreme Court decision outlawing separate educational facilities for African American people, write your own three reasons why "separate but equal" has no place in American schools.

> *I have a dream that one day my four children will live in a nation where they will not be judged by the color of their skin but by the content of their character.*
> —SPOKEN BY MARTIN LUTHER KING, JR.,
> IN HIS "I HAVE A DREAM SPEECH" IN
> WASHINGTON, DC, AUGUST 1963

Suggestion: Write your own "I Have a Dream" speech in which you state three to five dreams you have that will make America an even better place to live than it is now.

Quotable Quotes from Women in History

Until recent times, the words of women were rarely quoted except within the circles of the women who stated them. Yet, women, like men, also spoke out for freedom and liberty, both for themselves and for others. Following is a sampling of women's words with suggestions for written responses. Teacher's can of course add their own favorites to these.

> *In the new code of laws which I suppose it will be necessary for you to make, I desire you would remember the ladies and be more generous and favorable to them than your ancestors. Do not put such unlimited power into the hands of the husbands. Remember men would be tyrants if they could.*
> —ABIGAIL ADAMS IN A LETTER TO HER HUSBAND
> JOHN, A DELEGATE AT THAT TIME TO THE
> CONTINENTAL CONGRESS, JULY 1776

Suggestion: Write a letter to Abigail Adams telling her whether or not you agree with her words to her husband. Before you write, research what she means by "be more generous and favorable" and why she worries that "men would be tyrants."

> *It is not easy to be a pioneer—but oh, it is fascinating! I would not trade one moment, even the worst, for all the riches in the world.*
> —ELIZABETH BLACKWELL, WHO AFTER MANY YEARS OF
> APPLYING AND BEING REJECTED BECAUSE SHE
> WAS A WOMAN, WAS FINALLY ADMITTED TO THE
> PHILADELPHIA MEDICAL SCHOOL IN 1850

Suggestion: Write a letter to Elizabeth Blackwell, congratulating her on getting into medical school. Then tell her two or three reasons why you admire her pioneering spirit.

> *Men their rights and nothing more; women their rights and nothing less.*
> —SUSAN B. ANTHONY, THE WOMAN'S RIGHTS
> ACTIVIST, IN HER BOOK *THE REVOLUTION*

Suggestion: Write a list of rights that you believe belong to both women and men. If you think that there are different rights for women and men, write a separate list.

> *Science may have found a cure for most evils; but it has found no remedy for the worst of them all—the apathy of human beings.*
> —HELEN KELLER, SPEAKER, EDUCATOR, AND
> WRITER, IN HER BOOK *MY RELIGION*

Suggestion: Apathy means indifference to what happens to others. Imagine that you are a scientist working on a cure for apathy. Write a report telling of your work and your progress in making people more concerned with the welfare of others.

> *Of my two 'handicaps,' being female put many more obstacles in my path than being black.*
> —SHIRLEY CHISHOLM, THE FIRST BLACK WOMAN
> TO REPRESENT NEW YORK STATE IN THE
> HOUSE OF REPRESENTATIVES, 1968

Suggestion: Define what you think Shirley Chisholm means by "handicaps." Then create two lists. In one write the "handicaps" of being Black; in the other list, write the "handicaps" of being female. Then create a third list telling how a person might fight their way out of these "handicaps."

Other Quotable Quotes

Following are Quotable Quotes that can be presented to students at times when they seem appropriate to a specific lesson. Students can respond to these statements in a variety of ways. They may have had a personal experience they can relate to the quote, or the quote may evoke a personal reaction. They may want to collect their own Quotable Quotes to use as introductions to their writings as is often customary with published works. Quotable Quotes can be posted in the room, can serve as the focus or theme for bulletin boards, and can be used as discussion starters.

> *I never worry about action, only inaction.*
> —WINSTON CHURCHILL

> *Seize the day. Make your life extraordinary.*
> —THE DEAD POETS SOCIETY

> *Only those who dare to fail greatly can ever achieve greatly.*
> —ROBERT KENNEDY

> *The best and most beautiful things in the world cannot be seen or even touched. They must be felt by the heart.*
> —HELEN KELLER

> *Two roads diverged in a wood and I took the one less traveled by, and that has made all the difference.*
> —ROBERT FROST

LINKING TO THE COMPUTER

For finding Quotable Quotes, the Internet is a magic resource. Merely by searching for quotations or using the search term *quotations of famous people,* hundreds of items appear, many of them categorized by special topic as done in this chapter. One can find Quotable Quotes from all subject areas and from people of the past and present from all over the world. Of course, books also are a source for quotations, so teachers may want to encourage students to locate quotations on the Internet within their original source.

For using the computer more interactively, ask students to exchange their own significant Quotable Quotes on chat room forums that they set up for this purpose. Most students enjoy sharing their "wisdom," especially when they give their chat room friends permission to use their quotes in school writing and get back writing in which they are quoted.

CHAPTER 12

Personifications and Interactions

Subject Area Conversations

It's all in how you look at things.

—Alec in *The Phantom Tollbooth*

PERSONIFICATIONS AND INTERACTIONS:
A NEW POINT OF VIEW

Alec, the character in *The Phantom Tollbooth* who grows down (rather than up), teaches the young character Milo the importance of point of view. Pointing to a bucket of water, he tells Milo that "from an ant's point of view it's a vast ocean, from an elephant's just a cool drink, and to a fish, of course, it's home. So, you see, the way you see things depends a great deal on where you look at them from" (Juster 1989, 108).

The Personifications and Interactions writing strategy shows students how to write from another person's point of view or an object's point of view by assuming the persona of that person or object. A writer can assume the role of an historic person writing to another historic person across time, such as Betty Friedan writing to Susan B. Anthony, or as one literary character writing to another literary character; for example, Portia (from the *Merchant of Venice*) writing to Katherine (of *Taming of the Shrew*). Or Portia could write to Susan B. Anthony. An object can write to another object so that a triangle describes itself to a square, the element gold describes itself to the element iron, and the digestive system exchanges information with the nervous system.

In using personification as a writing strategy, the writer thinks of herself or himself as an historic person or person of note, a literary character, an animal, or an inanimate object. In the guise of a new persona, the writer writes to another writer (classmate) who has assumed a similar historic, literary, animal, or inanimate persona, creating writing interactions. When students engage in Personifications and Interactions, they must deeply know who or what they are to impersonate, so to speak, and they must be able to take the point of view of that personification. Through Personifications and Interactions, students are involved in both the subject area and the creative process.

PERSONIFICATIONS AND INTERACTIONS ACROSS THE CURRICULUM

This strategy can be and should be used from the primary grades through high school as a way of imparting information, opinions, beliefs, and narrative events. It gives students the opportunity to "get out of themselves" and understand a different point of view, either human or inanimate, and allows the students to write seriously or humorously. By assuming a new persona, writers must operate under the concept of "know thyself" in order to present or state their point of view to someone or something else. In addition, the strategy Personifications and Interactions lends itself particularly to letter writing.

Personifications and Interactions in the Primary Grades

For young students, assuming another identity is natural and easy. A student can be a storybook character, a flower talking to an animal, or a teacher speaking to her class. Because of the ease that many students have with role playing, they can write fluently and creatively from another point of view. A simple way to begin is with letter writing in which one student chooses to be a storybook character writing to another student role playing a different storybook character. By using letter writing, the students create an address and follow the conventions of friendly correspondence as illustrated in the following letter in which Boy Blue writes to Bo-Peep.

Boy Blue
4 Meadow Lane
Corn Row, Iowa 54321

Bo Peep
6 Shepherd Drive
Sheeptown, Oklahoma 87654

Dear Bo,

I just heard from Jack and Jill that you lost your sheep. I am so sorry. I know how you must feel because I once lost my cows. I fell asleep and when I woke up the cows were gone. But my friend Jack Horner told me to not worry. Cows always come home, he said. So I think you shouldn't worry either. Your sheep will come home and they will be so happy to see you that they will be wagging their tails and making happy sounds like baaaa. Write to me as soon as you find your sheep and tell me what happened.

Your friend,

Boy Blue

In the following letter, the student is a dog who has just had a fight with the cat from around the corner.

T. J. Rover

18 Canine Circle

Petsville, Washington 24680

Willy Cat

21 Feline Alley

Petsville, Washington 24680

Dear Willy,

My master told me to write this letter and tell you that I am sorry for chasing you around the yard. I know that I woke you up when you were taking a nap and that is why you were so angry with me. But you didn't have to scratch me so hard. I only wanted to play with you, but you thought I wanted to hurt you. Maybe you can come over to my yard tomorrow. Just crawl under the fence and come to where my doghouse is. I will save you some of my food. I always have some chicken and beef and even a bone. If you like those things we can share them. My master put some burning medicine on my scratches, but now they feel better. Write soon and let me know if you will visit.

Your friend,

T.J.

This third example is an odd number writing to an even number.

I. M. Odd

135 Uneven Road

Numbertown, New Jersey 97531

TAXONOMY SHEET

Object-to-Object Taxonomy for Personifications and Interactions

Directions: Imagine that you are one of the items in this Taxonomy. Write a letter to the adjoining item telling as much as you can about yourself.

A	apple/orange
B	ball/bat
C	centimeter/inch
D	dime/nickel
E	
F	foot/hand
G	
H	hot/cold
I	inch/foot
J	
K	
L	light bulb/candle
M	microscope/telescope
N	number/letter
O	ocean/river
P	pencil/pen
Q	
R	rain/snow
S	shoe/sock
T	tent/cabin
U	
V	violin/clarinet
W	water/sand
X	
Y	
Z	

Figure 12.1

U. R. Even
44 22nd Street
Double Village, Arkansas 86422

Dear Ms. Even:

I am very happy that you are moving next door to me. For a long time I have only lived with odd numbers such as 11, 13, 15, and 17. Whenever we wanted to split up, there was always one number left over. No one was happy. But now that you are here we won't have that problem. Your numbers will easily fit in between us so 2 can be between 1 and 3 and 6 can be between 5 and 7 and 9 can be between 8 and 10. We will all have fun together, especially when we play our favorite games—adding and subtracting. Please write soon and tell me as much about yourself as you can.

Very sincerely,
I. M. Odd

Keep in mind that for students to assume the persona of these items, they must have read about them or discussed them thoroughly.

Personifications and Interactions is a strategy that also helps students develop a deep understanding of what a word can mean. For example, if the student personifies an orange, and writes to a student personifying an apple, the student as an orange must know its full characteristics and so, too, must the student responding as an apple. It may be helpful depending on the students' experience with personification to use a Defining Format prior to writing a letter. They can define themselves on the Defining Format to get a stronger understanding of those features and characteristics that characterize the animal or inanimate object (e.g., What is an orange?). If the students are writing as an historic person, they can set up a Biographic Format (e.g., Who was Harriet Tubman?). For a literary character, they can complete a Character Profile. In addition, teachers can set up a Taxonomy of objects that could write to other objects or a Taxonomy of literary characters that could in turn write to other literary characters. Figure 12.1 shows an example of an Object-to-Object Taxonomy developed by a third grade class.

Another effective way to use personification as a springboard for writing is for the student to assume the identity of one of the characters of a story and write a journal in the voice of that character. Figures 12.2 and 12.3

show two examples, one using the story *The Ugly Duckling* by Hans Christian Andersen and the other using the story *Wagon Wheels* by Barbara Brenner.

My Life as an Ugly Duckling

Directions: Imagine that you are the "Ugly Duckling." Keep a journal that tells about your sad and difficult days. Use the starters below to help you write your journal. Write two or three sentences after each starter.

Today was the first day of my life and nothing went right.

_____

This morning a hunter's dog almost attacked me.

_____

Since everyone thinks I'm so ugly, I will run away and go out into the wide world.

_____

Figure 12.2

Journal Based on the Story *Wagon Wheels* by Barbara Brenner

Directions: Imagine that you are a girl or boy in the pioneer days. Your mom or dad has left you and a younger sister alone to take care of the house for a few days. Keep a journal of what happens during the time your parent is away. Here is a plan for you to follow or you can use your own writing plan.

Monday—Mom (or Dad) has to leave us alone for five days.

(Tell why and where she [or he] must go.)

Tuesday—Today I had to do many chores. (Tell what you did.)

Wednesday—This was a scary day. (Tell the scary things that happened.)

Thursday—My little sister got sick. (Tell what happened and how you took care of her.)

Friday—Mom (or Dad) will be home tonight. (Tell what you're doing to get the house ready.)

Figure 12.3

Personifications and Interactions in the Middle Grades

Students in the middle grades enjoy and benefit from assuming Personifications and doing writing activities similar to the ones described for primary students. For example, the Taxonomy shown in figure 12.1 could be adapted for older students by changing the type of items listed. In addition to the items listed there, teachers and students can create Taxonomies of Personifications and Interactions from mathematics, science, social studies, literature, and other areas of the curriculum. Students might create a Taxonomy of Career-to-Career in which a veterinarian is paired with an ecologist. Or the students might set up a Taxonomy of

Literary Characters who would write to other literary characters. Following are suggestions that can easily be modified or expanded as appropriate to meet the students' needs and interests.

Animal Job Application

Following a unit of study on animals (e.g., rain forest, jungle, domestic), students complete a template in which they personify an animal seeking a human-type job (see Figures 12.4 and 12.5). After filling out the application, students can write letters of reference or expand the information given about education and qualifications.

Animal Job Application

1. Full Name

2. Social Security Marking

3. Address (Habitat, Region)

4. Position Wanted   5. Phone Number

6. Education and/or Past Experience

7. Qualifications (List skills or experiences that you believe qualify you for this job)

8. References (List people or animals we can contact, other than family)

9. Availability (Starting date and scheduling preferences)

Figure 12.4

Animal Job Application

1. Full Name   Leo Panthera, aka Lion

2. Social Security Marking   Paw

3. Address (Habitat, Region)

    40 High Plain Road, PO Den 312, Central Africa

4. Position Wanted   5. Phone Number

    Security Guard for Home, Bank, Office, or School   1-800-3JUNGLE

6. Education and/or Past Experience

    Cub Scout, Big Cat High School, Lion University, Apprentice to Chief of Pride

                                                    (continued)

Figure 12.5

7. Qualifications (List skills or experiences that you believe qualify you for this job)

Superb roaring ability, sharp tearing teeth, ferocious physical appearance, great stamina

8. References (List people or animals we can contact, other than family)

Clyde Beatty, Supervisor of Lion Tamers, Barnum & Bailey Circus, Sarasota, FL

9. Availability (Starting date and scheduling preferences)

Immediately after spring mating season. Prefer daytime hours.

Figure 12.5 (continued)

Teachers can easily combine this strategy with the teaching of letter writing by using imaginative ideas drawn from both subject area topics and literature. Figure 12.6 shows an example in which intermediate students prepare for assuming the identity of an animal or a different character.

Comparing Goats and Sheep

First, students prepare a chart showing both the similarities and differences between goats and sheep (see Figure 12.6).

Characteristics	Goats	Sheep
Looks	· short tail · long hollow horns directed up · cloven-hoofs · males have beards	· short tail · spiral horns · cloven-hoofs · no beards
Eating Habits	grass, leaves, small plants	grass
Capabilities	· climbs rocks and mountains · makes flying leaps · lands with both feet close together	· good runners and climbers on hills
Product for Humans	Angora wool, mohair wool, cashmere wool, leather, milk, cheese, meat	merino wool, lambs wool, carpet wool, fur coats, milk, cheese, meat
Other Uses	· pets · pullers of carts	· pets · pack animals for carrying goods
Habitats	· Western U.S. (Arizona, Texas, Wyoming) · Russia, India, France · high mountain areas and almost everywhere else	· Western U.S. · Russia, India, Great Britain · Australia, New Zealand · low mountain areas and almost everywhere else
Other Information	· babies are called kids · female is a nanny · male is a buck or billy goat	· babies are called lambs · female is an ewe · male is a ram

Figure 12.6

The teacher and students then review this information prior to writing a letter. For example, using the information in Figure 12.6, the following information would be reviewed:

Both sheep and goats have hair or wool that is good for making rugs. But sheep and goats are also different kinds of animals. They have different looks, different types of wool or hair, and different eating habits. They may also live in different places.

Students then pretend they are either a goat or a sheep. Students who assume the identity of a goat write to a sheep telling it about their looks (i.e., appearance), wool or hair, eating habits, and where they live. Students who assume the identity of a sheep write to a goat about the same type of information. Figure 12.7 shows a sample writing template for writing such a letter.

Following is an example of a letter-writing assignment using the strategy of personification based on Greek mythology. This example is based on the story of the competition between the goddess Athena and the mortal Arachne. Students are presented with a brief summary of the story and two letter-writing options as shown in Figure 12.8.

A post-reading writing activity based on the story *Hatchet* by Greg Paulsen is shown in Figure 12.9. This story is told through the words of the only visible character, Brian Robeson, a boy of about twelve years old, from divorced parents, who is going to visit his father living in the Canadian North Woods. Through Brian's words, the reader learns about both his parents and his relationship with them. *Hatchet* is a wonderfully written story about survival and lends itself to letter writing interactions that urge students to think empathetically about the character and his relationships with others.

Setting Up a Letter

Following is an example of what information goes where in a letter. Note that examples are written in parenthesis for each part of the letter.

Your Name   (B. B. Black Sheep)

Your Address   (12 Wide Ranch Lane, Adelaide, Australia)

Write to

Name of Goat   (T. J. Nanny Goat)

Address   (14 Mountainside Drive, Rocky Hill, Arizona)

Dear _____,

(Body of Letter)

Sincerely,

Your (Sheep) Name

Figure 12.7

Arachne's Plea

The Greek goddess Athena was famous for her skill in weaving and she allowed no mortal to surpass her in this skill. However, a young mortal woman named Arachne challenged Athena to compete with her and Athena accepted the challenge. Although Arachne's weaving was as beautiful and as brilliantly executed as Athena's, the jealous goddess was angered both by Arachne's defiance and ability. With her superior power, Athena punished Arachne by changing her into a spider, thereby forcing her to spin eternally and from threads that came from her own body.

Imagine that you are either Arachne or Athena.

If you are Arachne, write a letter to Athena asking her forgiveness and begging her to return you to human form. In your letter, do all of the following:

- Praise and compliment Athena for her skill and her positive characteristics as a goddess.

- Tell Athena of your mistake in challenging a goddess of such esteem.

- Make Athena offers of loyalty, gifts, devotion, obedience, or whatever else you think would placate her and make her forgive you.

If you are Athena, write a letter to Arachne either holding firm to your punishment or else forgiving her. If you continue your punishment, give her three reasons for your decision. If you choose to forgive her, demand three tasks that she must do and describe these tasks in detail.

Figure 12.8

Personification of a Literary Character

Think of yourself as Brian, Mrs. Robeson, or Mr. Robeson and write a letter to one of the other characters. For example, as Mrs. Robeson, you can write to either Brian or Mr. Robeson. In this letter, share your wishes, fears, disappointments, and love or anger. Be as specific as you can so that the "person" receiving your letter understands your feelings.

From the story *Hatchet*, select the character you wish to be. Then complete the following chart before you write, by listing your wishes, fears, and emotions or feelings. For example, you might wish your "parents got back together," you might fear that you'll never be rescued, you might be filled with feelings or emotions of sadness, hopelessness, or worry. Use the story to help you decide what to list and also add your own ideas.

I am writing as _____

I am writing to _____

My Wishes

My Fears

My Emotions

Figure 12.9

Following are several writing samples created by students. All portray the writer's emotional reactions to this story.

Dear Mary,

Where is my son Brian? He should have been here days ago. I'll take you to court if you have him. I get him over the summer and you get him over spring, winter, and fall. So that means you'd better have him. You know I'm as mad as I can get. I've been waiting for him instead of going to work, so now I'm short of money. And don't say he came!

Your ex-husband,

Harry

Dear Harry,

The reason I am writing is to tell you why we got divorced. You may or may not know, but I was seeing another man. I didn't want this to go on and hurt you, so I asked for a divorce. Did Brian get there? I gave him a present—a brand new shiny hatchet that I found in the attic. I think it was yours—the one you used for cutting wood. So far, things are not going well with Frank (my new hated boyfriend). He comes home very late and drunk. I was thinking of breaking up with him. I am sorry I broke up with you. I guess I was a little crazy. So how about it? That would be really nice.

Sincerely,

Marge

Dear Mom,

I hope you're not wondering why I am not at Dad's house. Well, while I was in the plane, the pilot had a heart attack and died. I flew and landed the plane all by myself. I crashed in a lake.

I don't have much food. All I eat is fish, raspberries, and turtle eggs. A black bear showed me where to find blackberries. I made a fire when a porcupine came where I was sleeping and hit me in the leg with its tail. Then I threw my hatchet on the stone wall and made sparks. I realized then that I can make a fire.

My biggest fear is staying alive in the Canadian wilderness. I've already been here for forty-seven days. Mom, can you please get searchers to search for me? If you and Dad had never gotten a divorce, this would have never happened to me.

Love always,

Brian

Using Personification and Interactions in Content Areas—Social Studies

The Personifications and Interactions strategy lends itself well to content areas, such as social studies. For example, in a study of the American colonies, the students would can set up Taxonomies on words related to early American colonies. Then the students can complete a Profile of a colony (see Figure 12.10) and imagine they were one of the colonists writing to another such person in a different colony (see Figure 12.11).

Profile of a Colony

Name of Colony _____

Location _____

First Settlers _____

Reasons for Settlements _____
_____

Leaders Associated with Colony _____
_____

Major Products or Industries of Colony _____
_____

Types of Governance _____

Attitudes toward Outsiders
_____

Major Occupations or Work of Males
_____

Major Occupations or Work of Females
_____

Other Information
_____

Figure 12.10

Colonist Writes to Colonist

Directions: Imagine that you are a colonist in one of the thirteen American colonies. Write to a friend who lives in another colony. Tell about your life in the colony. Use your Colony Profile for facts and your Taxonomy to discuss work and occupations.

Format of Letter

Your "Colonial" Name

Address in Your Colony

Name of Your Colony

Your Friend's "Colonial" Name

Address of Your Friend

Name of Your Friend's Colony

Dear _____,

Tell why you are writing (e.g., So much has happened since I last wrote to you . . .)

Give news about your family and what each family member is doing to help each other in a new settlement.

Tell about important happenings in the colony—decisions of leaders, conflicts with Indians or other peoples, new arrivals, or other newsworthy events.

Ask your friend questions about her or his life in a different colony.

Invite your friend to visit. Give suggestions about how to travel and how to get to your house.

Sign off with a friendly greeting.

Figure 12.11

Using Personifications and Interactions in Content Areas—Mathematics

In the middle school, students can use Personifications and Interactions to write about different types of numbers (see Figure 12.12).

Personification of Mathematical Terms

Directions: Imagine you are a mathematical process, procedure, operation, or number in a mathematics department. Write a memo or letter to a member of your department explaining who you are and how you operate.

Figure 12.12

Following is an example written by a middle school student.

B. A. Fraction, Ph. D.
4/5 Denominator Road
Mathville, Montana 4/5,3/4,1/2,1/3

R. U. Whole Number, Ed. D.
419 Digit Lane
Numberland, Nebraska 11,5,4,8

Dear Dr. Whole Number:
Hi! I am a part of a whole. I have a numerator as well as a denominator. I have to be reduced to lowest terms. I can play around by being a percent or a decimal. I like to be written as a mixed number because then I am both a digit and a fraction. However, sometimes I am an improper fraction when my numerator is larger than my denominator. When this happens, I am very uncomfortable and ask to be changed into a mixed number. Write back soon and tell me about yourself.
Your friend,
B. A. Fraction, Ph. D.

LINKING TO THE COMPUTER

One interactive relationship to the computer is the chat room, which many students use for socializing. Students can find a "buddy," or chat room partner and set up a Personification and Interaction "chat." In such a chat, each student would personify a historic person, literary character, animal, or object (preferably from their curriculum) and converse as that personification. To make this a learning experience, the students would have to express detailed information about themselves and perhaps tell of unusual or interesting events in their lives as that persona. If possible, students can print out their chats and share them with other students.

The class also may be able to establish a class home page or Web site where students could enter information about themselves in a particular persona and request responses from other personae. The requested information should relate to important facts or interesting anecdotes or events so that the students are engaged in an exchange and exploration of ideas.

taxonomies

composing with
keywords

metacognition

defining format

profiles
and frames

who's who?

reasons, causes,
results

where in
the world

premises, premises

quotable quotes

personifications
and interactions

*morphology,
etymology,
and grammar*

Morphology, Etymology, and Grammar
Words for Grammar and History

*They've a temper, some of them—particularly verbs:
they're the proudest—adjectives you can do anything
with, but not verbs—however, I can manage the whole
lot of them! Impenetrability! That's what I say!*
Humpty Dumpty in *Through the Looking Glass*
(Lewis Carroll 1965, 94)

TRADITIONAL SCHOOL GRAMMAR—SUBJECT IN A TIME WARP

The teaching of English grammar is stuck in a time warp based on eighteenth-century notions of what English should be rather than what English is. In the delightful and well-researched book *The Mother Tongue: English and How It Got That Way*, Bill Bryson states:

> English grammar is so complex and confusing for the one very simple reason that its rules and terminology is based upon Latin—a language with which it has precious little in common. . . . Making English grammar conform to Latin rules is like asking people to play baseball using the rules of football. It is patently absurd. (1990, 137)

Yet, when established linguists and other language experts point out the foolishness of trying to teach English grammar through Latin, many teachers reply that they have to follow the English book and even if the book is wrong, they have no choice since the students will have to take a test and answer wrongly stated information correctly.

Before reading on, take the following test on nouns. Does the traditional grammar book definition of a noun make sense today?

True or False?

Directions: A noun (according to traditional school grammar books) is a person, place, or thing. Underline the nouns in this passage. Then decide which nouns are *persons*, which are *places*, and which are *things* and list them in the table that follows the passage.

The new **employee** displayed her **anger** and **indignation** to her **boss.** "We've never had a **discussion** about my **terms** of **employment.** First, you make me an **offer** of a **salary;** then you decide to give me only a **commission.** Finally, you ask me to hand in my **resignation.** Your **behavior** shows **arrogance, indifference,** and total **lack** of **concern** to my **needs.** I have two **plans:** to look for another **job** immediately or to file **suit** against your **company.**"

Persons	Places	Things

Figure 13.1

Frustrated with the previous task? Try this one and see if it works any better.

True or False?

Directions: Many school grammar books classify words such as *up, out, before,* and *down* as prepositions, meaning that they indicate the location of the noun that follows it (e.g., *in* the sky; *up* to the house; *before* the class). Underline all the verbs that are followed by words that traditionally are classified as prepositions. What "part of speech" would you call these words that come after the verbs?

"**Wake up**," Mother **called out**. "**Clean up** your room before you go to school. I have to **hurry up** so that I can **back out** my car from the garage. Dad needs to **get out** early for his meeting."

Figure 13.2

Teaching grammar serves a useful purpose when it is taught for the purpose of helping students write (or possibly speak) better. However, forcing students to classify words such as *anger, discussion, possibility, industrialization* as "things" will in no way improve their word knowledge or their writing. Underlining the subject once and the predicate twice in the sentence "It is raining" can hardly improve a student's communication skills. Yet, in hundreds of classrooms, teachers cling to these labels and display products purchased at teachers stores that tell students these shibboleths of nouns, verbs, adjectives, and sentences. No wonder Humpty says, "They've a temper" (Carroll 1965, 94).

Without throwing out grammar, teachers can provide lessons and activities that encourage students to think about English *as it is* and show students how to create meaningful, *information-bearing* sentences in their writing. Through the activities and strategies of Categories of Nouns, Categories of Verbs, Sentence Stretchers, Morphology and Etymology, Defining Format, and ABC Stories, students can learn how words (parts of speech) can be accurately categorized and understood and how the word-order rules of English provide writers a structure for expanding ideas and literary quality.

Categories of Nouns

This activity can be taught with students starting in the third grade and used throughout all grade levels as an extension of vocabulary building. Students divide their papers into four columns, one marked Persons, one marked Places, one marked Objects, and the last one marked Other. The teacher calls out a list of specific nouns and asks the students to place each noun in its appropriate category. When completed, the chart looks like the one shown in figure 13.3.

Persons	Places	Objects	Other
author	avenue	axe	anger
barber	building	ball	behavior
child	church	card	Christmas
designer	den	dress	dog
electrician	eatery	emerald	effort
friend	farm	fork	friendliness
grandparent	garden	glass	generosity
helper	home	hat	housework
Indian	igloo	iron	intelligence
janitor	jail	jacket	judgment

Figure 13.3

Even when students are not sure about the meanings of the words that are not persons, places, or objects, they usually know that such words are not "things," a term many school grammarians use as a substitute for the word *object.* When students are asked to classify those word in the Other list, they easily say that *dog* is an animal and *Christmas* is a holiday, and some students realize that *anger* is a feeling or emotion. Although some school grammar books have added "idea" as part of the definition of noun, this doesn't automatically enable students to identify *dog, anger,* or *Christmas,* as a person, place, thing, or idea, since *dog* and *anger* can hardly can be thought of as ideas and *Christmas* is undoubtedly much deeper than an idea.

Using the table format, teachers can expand the classification of nouns to include other categories, such as animals, emotions, and school subjects. After a while, the list of nouns might look like the one shown in figure 13.4. Note that the taxonomy format of listing the letters vertically has been added to the table.

TAXONOMY SHEET

	Persons	Places	Objects	Animals	Emotions	Subjects	Other
A	author	avenue	ax	ape	anger	art	action
B	barber	building	ball	bear		biology	beauty
C	child	church	card	cheetah	concern	carpentry	charm
D	designer	den	dress	dog	desire	design	depth
E	educator	eatery	emerald	eagle	envy	education	energy
F	friend	farm	fork	fox	fear		finality
G	grandma	garden	glass	goat	gladness	geometry	greed
H	helper	home	hat	hare	happiness	health	helplessness
I	Indian	igloo	iron	iguana	indignation	ichthyology	inaction
J	janitor	jail	jacket	jaguar	joy		joke
K	kid	kennel	kettle	kangaroo	kindness	kinetics	karma
L	leader	laundry	lamp	lion	love	literature	lesson
M	master	market	mirror	monkey	misery	mathematics	melody
N	neighbor	Norway	nutcracker	newt		nutrition	nod
O	owner	orchard	opener	owl		ornithology	opportunity
P	pal	pool	pin	panda	pleasure	psychology	position
Q	queen	quagmire	quilt	quail		quiltmaking	quest
R	runner	restaurant	ring	rabbit		radiology	rumor
S	student	school	sock	skunk	sympathy	science	song
T	teacher	tent	table	tiger	terror		temper
U	umpire		umbrella	unicorn			unit
V	violinist	vineyard	vase	vixen			vision
W	waitress	wadi	watch	whale	worry	weaving	wisdom
X	xylophonist	Xanadu	xylophone	xenotype			x-factor
Y	youth	yard	yardstick	yak			youthfulness
Z	zookeeper	zoo	zither	zebra		zoography	zero

Figure 13.4

Before continuing to the next group of noun categories, students compose sentences using the strategy Composing with Keywords, as described in chapter 3. Students select three words from three different categories of which one category should be from the "Other" column. They then compose a sentence using the three words in *one* sentence, with the option to change the forms of the words if necessary. Here are several examples taken from students in different grades.

My grandma bought me a monkey that had a bad temper.
I get a lot of pleasure when my teacher tells me that I got an A in mathematics.

I sang a song of happiness to the queen.
There was a rumor that the skunk was in the restaurant.
Some students in my geometry class have a lot of wisdom.

By generating their own sentences, students not only learn about the variety of nouns but begin to use more advanced vocabulary and develop flexibility in their sentence composing skills. When nouns are "things," everything can be anything, with nothing much mattering.

Once students have an understanding of what a noun is, they are ready to learn about noun endings, called *affixes*. The most common of these affixes are *-ness -ion, -ment, -ence/ance, -ity,* and *-ism,* as shown in the following lists (see Figure 13.5), which were developed over time with students in the third grade and reviewed in the intermediate grades.

TAXONOMY SHEET
Noun Endings

	-ness	-ion	-ment	-ence/-ance	-ity	-ism
A	attractiveness	attention	advancement	attendance	activity	absolutism
B	boldness	bastion	bereavement	benevolence	brevity	Buddhism
C	carelessness	commotion	commitment	credence	creativity	Creationism
D	darkness	detention	department	difference	deity	Darwinism
E	eagerness	elation	engagement	exuberance		extremism
F	friendliness	fraction	fragment	forbearance	fragility	feudalism
G	gentleness	generation	government	governance	gratuity	gigantism
H	helpfulness	humiliation	harassment	hindrance	humanity	humanism
I	inventiveness	information	instrument	intelligence	individuality	individualism
J	judiciousness	juxtaposition	judgment	jurisprudence	joviality	Judaism
K	kindness					
L	loneliness	lamentation	ligament		lucidity	
M	maliciousness	motion	monument	magnificence	magnanimity	minimalism
N	neatness	notion			nobility	nepotism
O	openness	operation		opulence	opportunity	opportunism
P	playfulness	perforation	parliament	permanence	perspicacity	populism
Q	quietness	question		quintessence	quantity	
R	ruthlessness	radiation	rudiment	radiance	radioactivity	rationalism
S	sweetness	situation	sentiment	significance	sensitivity	sensationalism
T	timeliness	temptation	temperament	temperance	timidity	Taoism
U	usefulness	usurpation	understatement		utility	utilitarianism
V	viciousness	variation		vehemence	veracity	
W	wastefulness		wonderment			
X						
Y						
Z	zealousness					Zoroastrianism

Figure 13.5

SkyLight Professional Development

These lists can be used for vocabulary and sentence development, with teachers emphasizing the formation or morphology of these words.

Categories of Verbs

The verb, like the noun, often is given short shrift as teachers tell their students that a "verb is a word of action." Sentences such as "Nothing exists" defy this explanation, but some teachers tell us that this sentence is about the "action of nonexistence." Or something like that. Indeed! It is difficult to convince teachers that they are teaching grammar from an eighteenth-century perspective, perhaps because they are unfamiliar with the vast body of literature on the English language written by distinguished linguists. Robert Claiborne, in *Our Marvelous English Tongue—The Life and Times of the English Language*, points out how the Latinists saddled "English with quite a few arbitrary rules" (1983, 186) and "literary prissiness" coming from their "attempt to jam English into the Procrustean bed of Latin rules, through an elaborate structure that managed to confuse some generations of schoolchildren" (186). Conventional teaching certainly has given a "temper" to the verbs by asking students to "parse" the English verb *love* as if it had the same structure as the Latin word *amare* with its elaborate forms of infinitive, gerunds, participles, subjunctives, past, present, future, and whatever else belonged to Latin, but not to English.

Students can become better writers through an introduction to the variety of verbs they need as writers. For example, in writing, they need to replace tired verbs such as *think, say,* and *go* with more varied, vivid words. Creating Taxonomies of vivid words gives students an extensive vocabulary to draw upon when writing.

As an opening activity, students from the third grade on can create four-column charts of verbs similar to the one used for nouns. After creating the chart and titling it (e.g., Verbs of . . .), students draw a human figure including a head, neck, and body in the first column. They then title the other columns The Mind, Vocalization, and Locomotion. The teacher explains that verbs are words that often can be related to the body so that when someone says, "I think," "I imagine", or "I dream," that verb is in the mind. When someone says, "I speak," "I whisper," "I yell," that person is using verbs of vocalization. And when someone says, "I walk," "I gallop," "I ride," "I catapult," he or she is using verbs of locomotion.

As teachers guide the students in collecting categories of nouns, they similarly can guide students in collecting categories of verbs. A collection (in progress) is shown in Figure 13.6.

TAXONOMY SHEET
Verbs of . . .

		The Mind	Vocalization	Locomotion
A		admire, appreciate, accept	announce, ask	amble
B		believe	babble, beg, berate, bellow	bound
C		consider, concentrate	converse, convince, cry	crawl, creep, catapult, careen
D		dream	demand, dialogue	drive, dance
E		envision	exhort, explain	
F		foresee, forget		fly
G		germinate	giggle, growl, greet	glide, gyrate
H		imagine, inquire	hum, harmonize, holler, howl	hop, hobble
I		investigate	interview	
J		judge	joke	jump
K		know		
L		love	laugh	leap, lumber
M		mull over	mention, murmur, mumble	meander
N		notice	narrate	navigate
O		overlook	orate	
P		plan. perceive, ponder	persuade, pray, plead	paddle, plow, prance
Q			question, query	
R		remember, respect, realize	retell, reply, request, rant	run, race, rocket
S		suppose, surmise	say, speak, sing, screech	skate, speed, slither, slide, skip, soar, scamper, scurry
T		think	tell, talk, trill	tiptoe
U		understand	utter	undulate
V		verify, visualize	vocalize	vault
W		wonder, wish, worry	whistle, whisper	walk, waddle
X				
Y		yearn	yell, yodel	
Z				zoom

Figure 13.6

Students, of course, can add to this collection and keep it in their folder or Taxonomy book for use when they are writing. From this collection of verbs of the Mind, Vocalization, and Locomotion, they can create other categories or Taxonomies, such as verbs of Caring and Feeling, Gesture and Body Language, Encounter, Disapproval and Displeasure, and others. The verb now is not simply a matter of action but of behaviors that may be mental, vocal, or physical.

Sentence Stretchers

Teachers can next move to showing students how verbs, nouns, and other word categories form the sentence structures of English. Using an activity called Sentence Stretchers, teachers can guide students in creating expanded sentences that also indicate major parts of speech. This activity requires the use of an eight-slot chart as shown in Figure 13.7, with the slots referring to the place where certain parts of speech are most likely to fit.

1	2	3	4	5	6	7	8
When	Determiner	Adjective	Animal	Verb of Locomotion	Adverb	Where	Punctuation
Early this Morning	several	colorful	giraffes	galloped	gracefully	over the mountains	[.]

Figure 13.7

To maximize students' understanding of Sentence Stretchers, the following procedures can be used:

- Provide students with legal-size paper and have them fold it horizontally into eight slots. Ask them to number each slot.

- Begin with the fourth slot and tell the students to enter the name of an animal and then make the word plural (wolf/wolves, bear/bears).

- Go to the fifth slot and enter a verb of locomotion. Keep the verb in the base form (*stalk, pounce, fly*).

- Go to slot 3. Enter an adjective. Make sure students avoid words such as nice or good and guide them towards words such as *dangerous, courageous, graceful, peaceful, fierce,* and so forth.

- Go to slot 2. Here the word *determiner* is used to determine the amount or number. A determiner can be an exact number such as three or it can be an inexact number represented by words such as *some, many, several, numerous,* or words such as "a pack of." (Make sure students do not confuse adjectives with determiners, since they each serve different purposes.)

- Go to slot 6. Ask students to enter an -*ly adverb*. An -ly adverb is an adjective to which -ly has been added (*angry/angrily, brave/bravely/ graceful/gracefully*).

- Go to slot 1. Now the student enters *when* this event occurred (*At the stroke of midnight*). The student must now go to slot 5 and check that the verb is in the right form or tense and change it if necessary (*dance/danced*).

- Go to slot 7 and enter *where (in the playground)*.

- Go to slot 8 and put in punctuation.

Once the students know the procedure, they can write an infinite number of expanded sentences while creating their own Taxonomies of Adjectives, Animals, Verbs of Locomotion, and Adverbs. Students also like to illustrate these sentences because they tend to be fantasy or simply ridiculous.

After students have practiced Sentence Stretchers using Verbs of Locomotion, proceed with two variations—one with Persons and Verbs of Vocalization and one with Persons and Verbs of the Mind using the arrangements shown in Figure 13.8 and 13.9.

1	2	3	4	5	6	7	8
When	Determiner*	Adjective	Person	Verb of Vocalization	Adverb	Where	Punctuation
Just as the meeting started	twenty	brilliant	students	chanted	wildly	in the assembly	[.]
Every evening	a group of	talented	actors	recite	gloriously	on the stage of the Globe theater	[.]

Figure 13.8

In the Sentence Stretcher that uses Verb of the Mind, use a six-slot chart such as the one shown in figure 13.9. The students complete the sentences with their own appropriate words.

1	2	3	4	5	6
When	Determiner*	Adjective	Person	From Where	Verb of the Mind
By late afternoon	several	scholarly	teachers	from my school	realized . . .
Last winter	a class of	courageous	children	living in Australia	decided . . .

Figure 13.9

Understanding "Parts of Speech" by Using Defining Format

The theme of this book—writing as learning—emphasizes that when students construct meanings through writing, they understand what they are trying to understand. So it is with explaining language, especially English, which has the largest known vocabulary of any of the world's languages, a vocabulary that is drawn from numerous other languages, and a grammar system that has developed and re-formed for over a thousand years. No wonder teachers are on slippery terrain when they try to explain English parts of speech. However, after students have explored aspects of the English language through the activities that have been previously suggested, they can then try to pin down some explanations though Defining Format. The examples shown in Figures 13.10–13.12 define noun, verb, and adjective—three terms, among others, that traditional school grammar books have failed to examine carefully or explain accurately.

* Note that the "slots" in Sentence Stretchers clearly indicate that not all words that precede nouns are adjectives. Determiners such as many, few, several, each, every, and similar words indicate amount and determine the singularity or plurality of the noun (each friend, many friends). Adjectives in English do not affect amount (one beautiful lamp, three beautiful lamps). Also, an adjective can be used to construct a sentence such as "The lamps are beautiful." But one cannot say, "The lamps are three."

DEFINING FORMAT
What Is a Noun in the English Language?

Question	Category	Characteristics
What is a noun? A noun is a	word that	1. names many categories, including: persons, places, objects, animals, emotions, and whatever can be named. 2. may have specific endings: -ion, -ment, -ence/-ance, -ness, -ity, -ism 3. may be singular or plural: girl-girls, mouse-mice, wolf-wolves, sheep-sheep, alumnus-alumni, addendum-addenda 4. may be formed from verbs: I played in a *play*. *Playing* is fun. 5. may be paired with a verb, but is distinguished by stress: I don't want to *subject* you to this *subject*. We have to *reject* all *rejects*. I have to *record* this note for the *record*.

Figure 13.10

DEFINING FORMAT
What Is an Adjective in the English Language?*

Question	Category	Characteristics
What is an adjective? An adjective is a	word that	1. compares or contrasts the quality or appearance of a noun: the beautiful (i.e., not ugly) dress; the brave (i.e., not cowardly) soldier; the white (i.e., not brown) horse 2. may add the inflections -er and -est: big, bigger, biggest 3. may be preceded by *more* or *most; less* or *least; quite, rather,* or *very* more dangerous, least dangerous quite dangerous, rather dangerous very dangerous 4. usually precedes the noun (fierce storms) or follows the "be" verb (The storms were fierce.)

Figure 13.11

		DEFINING FORMAT

What Is a Verb in the English Language?

Question	Category	Characteristics
What is a verb? A verb is a	word that	1. has four forms, also called its conjugation: 　a) base—I work, I will speak 　b) verb + <u>s</u>—She works. She speaks. 　c) past—She worked. She spoke. 　d) -ing—She is working. She was speaking. 2. may have a fifth form: -en — I have spoken. 3. forms the past in several ways: 　a) by dentalization—I worked [t]. She sighed [d]. He painted. [ad] 　b) by vowel change—We ran. They gave. He saw. She took. 　c) by null—Today I quit; yesterday I quit. 4. may "serve" in the noun or adjective position: 　Singing is fun for singing waiters. 　Traveling with traveling musicians makes a journey lively. 5. can be combined with other verbs to indicate time or tense: 　*We should have stayed in the park.* 　*From the moment I met her, I knew she was going to become my friend.*

Figure 13.12

Since the focus of this book is on writing instruction, only those aspects of school grammar that are directly related to helping students write are expanded upon. However, teachers and students can explore and discuss how English works and make up the rules after their explorations.

Morphology—The Study of the Formation of Words

Because of the need for students to have a knowledge of words in order to write and think, *Morphology* (and subsequently *Etymology*) is included among the strategies presented here. Morphology literally means the study *(-logo)* of the shapes *(morph-)* of words, a term derived from the Greek god of dreams, Morpheus, who had the ability to assume different shapes or appearances. English is a highly morphological language, meaning that a large number of its words can have affixes *(e.g., girl, girls, girlhood; play, playful, playfulness)* and only a very small number of words, called function words, do not affix *(e.g., the, but, and, some, all, this)*.

From the very beginning of reading instruction, teachers point out the plural formation of certain nouns and the verbs endings (technically called inflections). By second grade, therefore, most students are able to understand how "a word can have more than one form or shape" and are ready to learn Morphology. Again, the "slots" are headed by the terms *Noun, Verb, Adjective,* and *Adverb* (see Figure 13.13).

Morphology Chart			
Noun	Verb	Adjective	Adverb

Figure 13.13

The following is an example of how a teacher can use the word *play* to introduce Morphology or show how a word can have more than one form or shape. Teachers tell students to enter the word *play* in the column or slot labeled Verb in the grid. Then show how the four verb forms look or work by using the standard conjugation arrangement:

> I play.
> She/he plays.
> Yesterday we played.
> Now we are playing.

The Morphology Chart now looks like the one shown in Figure 13.14.

Morphology Chart—Verb Slot			
Noun	Verb	Adjective	Adverb
	play		
	plays		
	played		
	playing		

Figure 13.14

The forms can be named if desired: *base, verb-s, past, -ing*. The teacher then asks the students to recite the conjugation: I play; she plays; yesterday we played; now we are playing. He or she next tells them that an important way to recognize a verb is to say its forms since all verbs (except the "be" verb) have the same four forms.

Now comes an interesting "complication." Many words in English that are "born verbs" serve as nouns. One can see a *play* or see many *plays*. Students can enter the words *play* and *plays* in the noun slot and point out that while verbs will have four forms, nouns can only have two forms—singular and plural or "one and more than one." The chart looks like the one shown in figure 13.15.

Morphology Chart—Noun and Verb Slots			
Noun	Verb	Adjective	Adverb
play (1)	play		
plays (more than 1)	plays		
	played		
	playing		

Figure 13.15

Students finally complete the chart by adding the other forms of play: player/players, playful (adjective), playfully (adverb), and playfulness (noun). The compound forms may also be listed (see Figure 13.16).

Morphology Chart—Completed			
Noun	**Verb**	**Adjective**	**Adverb**
play	play	playful	playfully
plays	plays		
	played		
player	playing		
players			
playfulness			
playmate(s)			
playhouse(s)			
playground(s)			
playpen(s)			

Figure 13.16

It's best to follow up this introduction to *Morphology* by having the students collectively create a "Morphology sentence" such as "Six playful players who were full of playfulness playfully played with six playful playmates in the playhouse on the playground."

Using Morphology with students requires teachers to become aware of words with expansive morphologies and makes students aware of the various patterns of affixes (prefixes, suffixes, and inflections) in the English language. Figure 13.17 shows a Dual Taxonomy of words that can be used for Morphology lessons. It is divided into two levels of difficulty. Following this Taxonomy are examples of the morphologies of different words.

Verbs for Studying Morphology

The following verbs are those that can become other parts of speech such as nouns, adjectives, and adverbs. Teacher modeling for students or the students themselves select at least five of these verbs and set up a Morphology Chart for each word to show its different forms or parts of speech. If the verb forms any compound nouns, they are added to the Morphology.

	Level I	Level II
A	add, act, agree, attract	admire, anger, argue, appreciate, adore
B	boast, believe	beautify, befriend
C	care, comfort, copy	create, consider, civilize, circle
D	drive, delight, darken, disagree	decide, defend, decorate, design, depend
E	enjoy, eat, entertain, express	energize, endanger, endure, equal, enslave
F	fly, fool, free	frighten, finance, function
G	govern	generate, graph
H	help, hope	humanize, honor
I	imagine, improve, interest	invade, include, inquire, illustrate
J	jump	judge
K	know	
L	love	limit
M	move	multiply, manage, master, motivate
N	name	narrate, nationalize, note
O	open	organize, object, observe, occupy, offend
P	play, pay	progress, provide, possess, perceive
Q	question	qualify
R	rest, respect, run	reason, recognize, receive, reflect, repeat
S	speak, sweeten, serve, soften	sign, sympathize, secure, segregate
T	taste, transport, trick	terrify, transmit, tyrannize
U	use, understand	unite
V		value, vaccinate, verify, vibrate
W	wonder, waste, warm, wash, work	whiten
X, Y, Z		

Figure 13.17

Examples of Morphology Charts

Noun	Verb	Adjective	Adverb
addition	add	additional	additionally
additions	adds		
	added		
addend	adding		
addends			
additive			
additives			
addendum			
addenda			

Figure 13.18

Noun	Verb	Adjective	Adverb
belief	believe	believable	believably
beliefs	believes		
disbelief	believed	unbelievable	unbelievably
	believing		

Figure 13.19

Noun	Verb	Adjective	Adverb
defendant	defend	defensible	defensibly
defendants	defends	defensive	defensively
	defended	indefensible	indefensibly
defense	defending		
defenses			
defensiveness			

Figure 13.20

Noun	Verb	Adjective	Adverb
sign	sign		
signs	signs		
	signed		
signature	signing		
signatures			
signal	signal		
signals	signals		
signatory	signaled		
signatories	signaling		
significance		significant	significantly
	signify		
signification	signifies		
	signified		
	signifying		

Figure 13.21

The "Be" Verb

This verb differs from the other verbs of English in that it has a two-part system. The base word—be—has forms that contain the base itself:

> We will *be* there soon
>
> *Being* on time is important.
>
> I have *been* visiting my friends

Notice only three (of the five in this case) conjugation forms are used: be, being, been. In certain dialect forms, however, the other two forms are still in use:

> She *bes* good. (verb+*s*)
>
> We *beed* here a long time. (past dentalization)

These last two forms may be used in the speech dialects of certain communities and can be heard in the emerging speech of young students. Without making judgments about its use, one can see that the verb *be* follows the English verb conventions. However, it has a second strand— the forms *am, is, are, was, were*. These forms are currently more commonly used and are considered to be part of *standard* usage when matched to the appropriate noun or pronoun: *I am*, but not *I is*. Many middle schools and high schools find this discussion of usage fascinating. For further information and background on this topic refer to *The Story of English* (1986) and *The Mother Tongue* (1990).

Etymology

Etymology—the study of the origin of words—is also given much less attention than it merits in the study of English. From its roots in India, across Persia, up through the Germanic tribes into Scandinavia and across to Britain is one route towards the development of the English language. With the spread of Christianity and later the Renaissance, the lexicon of Greek and Latin along with the French of Normandy continued to enrich the language. English further expands in the New World while simultaneously spreading to Australia and into parts of Africa. So where in the world does the English language come from? Everywhere. Where in the world is the English language? Everywhere. Following are several activities that relate to the etymology of the English language.

Words and Their Stories

An informative book for young students is *10l Words and How They Began* by Arthur Steckler (1979). This is a good starting book to make students aware that words are born or come from other words or other languages. Teachers can supplement the reading by having students create lists of words they learned about from the story, or a Taxonomy of Words with a Story (Figure 13.22). If possible, provide students with the *Random House Unabridged Dictionary* (either the book or the CD-ROM), which tells the origin of most words. Another valuable book is the *Dictionary of Word Origins* by John Aton (1990). Then assign each student a word from the Taxonomy and write its "story" for compilation into an ABC book. You will find that once the students get hooked on etymology, they will become avid searchers of the origins of their names, their localities, the foods they eat, and the hundreds of other words that have a story.

Borrowings and Lendings

Counter to the advice of Polonius in Hamlet, English has heavily borrowed from other languages and, in turn, has loaned its own words freely—a process that linguistically enriches all those who speak it. As students prepare their Book of Word Stories, they will start to notice the variety of origins—French, Spanish, Greek, Latin, Hebrew, Native American, African, Arabic, and more. The Taxonomy activity shown in Figure 13.23 focuses on English words borrowed from India. Figure 13.24 shows words that come from ragtime and jazz, and words and place names from Native Americans are offered in Figure 13.25. Each of these Taxonomies can be used for Composing with Keywords or as the basis for research, discussion, and inclusion in numerous writing activities.

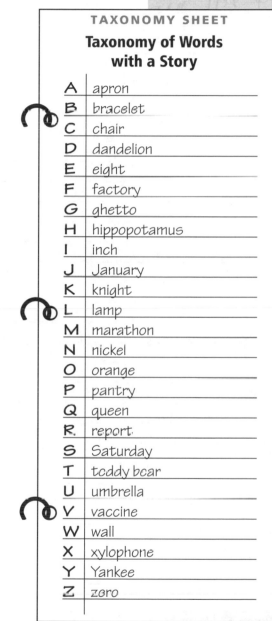

TAXONOMY SHEET

Taxonomy of Words with a Story

A	apron
B	bracelet
C	chair
D	dandelion
E	eight
F	factory
G	ghetto
H	hippopotamus
I	inch
J	January
K	knight
L	lamp
M	marathon
N	nickel
O	orange
P	pantry
Q	queen
R	report
S	Saturday
T	teddy bear
U	umbrella
V	vaccine
W	wall
X	xylophone
Y	Yankee
Z	zero

Figure 13.22

TAXONOMY SHEET
Passage from India

Directions: In the early 1600s, the British East India Company sent ships to India and by the end of the eighteenth century all major educational institutions in India used English as the primary language of instruction. But the English of India took on its own accents, idioms, and expressions. And, in turn, the native languages of the Indian people—Urdu, Hindi, Begali, Punjab—gave their own words to English. Check out the meanings of the words you don't know and tell "their story."

A |
B | brahmin, bungalow, bandanna
C | calico, coolie, curry, chintz, chutney, cummerbund
D | dhurrie, denim, dungarees
E |
F |
G | guru
H |
I |
J | jungle, Jute
K | karma
L |
M | Maharajah
N | Nirvana
O |
P |
Q |
R | Rajah, rupee
S |
T | toddy
U |
V | verandah
W |
X |
Y | yoga
Z |

Figure 13.23

TAXONOMY SHEET
And All that Jazz

Directions: From the early days of slavery to the present time, African Americans have used music to express their feelings, beliefs, and yearnings. From this music, English has enriched its vocabulary. Here are some of the words. Add others to this list and write a story about jazz and other music, using as many of these words as you need.

A |
B | blues, boogie-woogie, break dancing, be-bop
C | cool, cakewalk, chick
D |
E |
F |
G | groovy, gospel
H | hip, hip-hop, hepcat
I |
J | jam, jive, jitterbug
K |
L | latch on
M | mellow
N |
O |
P | pad
Q |
R | rap, riff
S | sharp, soul, solid, square
T |
U |
V |
W |
X |
Y |
Z |

Figure 13.24

TAXONOMY SHEET

Word Contributions from Native Americans

Following is a sampling of English words and place names that come from the American population who lived on the American continent before the arrival of the white settlers. Add your own words and place names to this list.

A	Alaska, Amagansett
B	
C	chipmunk, Connecticut
D	Delaware
E	
F	
G	
H	hominy, hogan
I	igloo
J	
K	kayak, Kissimmee
L	
M	moose, moccasin, Massachusetts
N	Neponset, Narragansett
O	opossum
P	powwow, papoose
Q	Quogue
R	raccoon
S	squash, squaw, skunk, Seattle, Seminole
T	teepee, totem, Tallahassee
U	Utah
V	
W	wigwam, wampum
X	
Y	
Z	

Figure 13.25

British English and American English

Students are always interested in comparing British words with American words, and this topic can be introduced in social studies, English, or language arts classes to show the great variety of words in the English language. The Taxonomy shown in Figure 13.25 contains some British versus American variations of the language.

TAXONOMY SHEET

A Taxonomy of American English Words and British English Words

Directions: Following are pairs of words that mean the same things. However, the first word is commonly used in the United States and the word in italics is used in the British Isles. Write a story in which you substitute the British words for the words you are more likely to use. For example, you might write about asking a *Bobby* to direct you to a place where you can rent a *flat* in a building with a *lift,* or get your *driving license,* or have a meal of fish and *chips.*

A | apartment *(flat)*

B | baby carriage *(pram),* beets *(beet roots),*

C | cookie *(biscuit),* crib *(cot),* cop *(Bobby),* candy *(sweets)*

D | driver's license *(driving license),* dishwashing liquid *(washing-up liquid)*

E | elevator *(lift),* eggplant *(aubergine),* expressway *(motorway)*

F | fries *(chips),* fire department *(fire brigade)*

G | garden hose *(hose pipe),* garbage can *(dustbin),* gasoline *(petrol)*

H | hood of a car *(bonnet),* hardware *(ironmongery)*

I |

J |

K |

L | long distance call *(trunk call),* lawyer *(barrister)*

M | mail *(post),* muffler *(silencer)*

N | nail polish *(nail varnish)*

O | out of style *(out of fashion)*

P | pail *(bucket),* period *(full stop),* pitcher *(jug),* potato chips *(crisps),* popsicle *(ice lolly)*

Q | quotation marks *(inverted commas)*

R | refrigerator *(fridge),* railroad car *(railroad carriage)*

S | soda *(fizzy drink),* subway *(underground or tube),* sidewalk *(pavement),* stove *(cooker)*

T | thread *(cotton),* traffic circle *(roundabout),* trunk of a car *(boot),* truck *(lorry),* two weeks *(fortnight),*

U |

V |

W | windshield wiper *(windscreen wiper)*

X |

Y |

Z |

Figure 13.26

ABC Stories

A frequent concern of teachers is that student writing lacks sentence variety. Teachers will exhort students to start their sentences with words other than *the, he,* or *and then* only to find their efforts are wasted, mainly because students can't think of other words. To help students realize the variety of words that they actually know and are capable of using, students can write ABC Stories—stories in which each sentence begins with a successive letter of the alphabet, as shown in the following example.

A long time ago, a Mother Pig told her three young pigs to build their own houses.

"**Build** your houses of the best materials you can," she advised.

Carl, the youngest Pig, chose to make his house of straw.

Damien, the middle Pig, thought that sticks would make a strong house.

Edgar, the oldest and wisest of the Pigs, knew that a house of bricks might last forever.

For a while Carl was safe in his house of straw.

"**Great!**" he thought.

"**Having** a straw house is cheap and pleasant."

Imagine his surprise when a Wolf came by one day and knocked on his door.

"**Jiggledy**, jiggledy, jiggledy, jiggledy jin,

Keep out of my way as I blow your house in."

Little Carl's straw house was blown into hundreds of pieces and scattered everywhere.

"**Making** a house of straw was not a good idea," thought Carl.

Obviously, with this activity, the student must use a variety of sentence starters—names, quotations, -ing verbs, exclamations, and whatever other form comes to mind. One way to start this activity is to ask students to write their first ABC stories based on a fairy tale they know well. After re-creating fairy tales, the students can write a variety of pieces as in the examples below:

Factual

Almost four hundred years ago, a group of people called Pilgrims were forced to leave England because of their religious beliefs.

But they were not sure of where to go.

Could they find a home outside of England they wondered.

During their search for a place to live, they heard about Holland.

Every English Pilgrim who had visited Holland came back and spoke of the kindness of the Dutch people.

Freedom of religion was important to the Pilgrims, so they hired a ship and brought their families to Holland.

Giving up their English ways, however, was not easy.

Hearing their children speak Dutch and forgetting their English made the Pilgrims unhappy.

"**It's** time to sail to the New World," their leaders advised.

"**Just** as God brought us to Holland, so God will deliver us to America."

Seventh grade student

Descriptive

In this assignment, students wrote a descriptive piece using an acrostic of a place they had visited. (In an acrostic, the letters of the topic or theme are used to begin each sentence.)

Marco Island is my favorite place to visit in the winter.

At night we have the most beautiful sunsets.

Rising early is important if you want to watch the seagulls playing.

Children splash and swim in the warm Gulf waters.

Of all the places in the world, I love Marco Island best.

Fourth grade student

Dialogue

In a Dialogue, students select a topic that interests them and create an acrostic using the letters of the topic to start each sentence. Following is an example of a teacher-created Dialogue about two people talking about soccer. The teacher can create a model for students before asking the students to work in pairs to create their own acrostic Dialogues.

Person 1   **S**ome day I hope to be the soccer champion of the world.

Person 2   **O**nly people born with strong legs can be a soccer champion.

Person 1   **C**hampions are made, not born.

Person 2   **C**razy ideas come into your head.

Person 1   **E**veryone can dream, and playing soccer is my dream.

Person 2   **R**emember that you will have to practice every day, seven days a week, and you can never give up.

LINKING TO THE COMPUTER

The Internet provides a great way to research the English language. Merely by going to Yahoo.com or any other search engine and typing the phrase *history of the English language,* students can find numerous references to sites on just about anything they would want to know about the topic. For example, the following topics are representative of the results of such a search:

American English   Grammar Usage and Style

Australian English   Middle English

Canadian English   Thesauruses

Dictionaries   Word of the Day

English as a Second Language   Words and Wordplay

Within each of these topics are numerous subtopics that can interest students from elementary through high school. By using the Internet, both teachers and students will discover a treasure of linguistic information.

CHAPTER 14

Writing as Editing

Writers Revisit

Editing . . . is making the text as easy as possible for the reader by presenting it in a manner that the reader is most likely to anticipate.

—*Writing and the Writer,* Frank Smith

GOOD WRITERS REVISIT THEIR WRITING—MANY TIMES

Most students, as fledgling writers, are puzzled about the need to "write it over again" and then after "writing it again," find they are disappointed when they fail to get the grade they think they deserve. Worse yet, for students, is to get back a paper "edited" by the teacher in red (or any other color). On the other hand, getting back a paper with few comments, even with a satisfactory grade, leaves students feeling empty. Such an experience may discourage students because they see that they have put in a lot of work for what appears to be very little reward. Teachers may also find the process less than satisfying, feeling burdened by reading and correcting unedited or poorly edited student writing. Every writer needs to revisit her or his paper, which means re-reading, re-stating, re-reading again, and re-writing again. And what is the reward for all this tedious work? It's called publishing, which in school means a wonderful piece of writing aesthetically produced by hand or on the computer, and appreciated and praised by peers, teachers, and hopefully, parents.

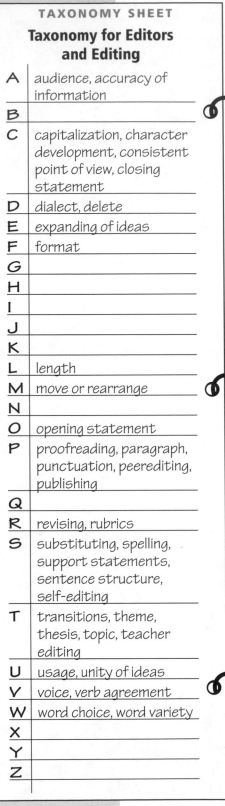

Figure 14.1

TEACHING "EDITING"—A.K.A. REVISING

Most teachers today recognize that writing and editing are an intertwined process—there can't be one without the other—and they assume, rightly, that as one teaches writing, one teaches editing. Teachers who have been deeply involved in teaching the writing process have undoubtedly incorporated many aspects of editing into their writing instruction, especially capitalization, punctuation, and the grammar of "incorrect usage." Students must think of all of their writing as starting with a *draft copy* (see chapter 1 for a discussion of the draft copy). At this phase in the writing process, students should always head their papers Draft Copy and leave room for editing, which means skipping lines or double spacing. The students know in advance that their first writing on a topic is a "work-in-progress" that may reach final or published copy. Some pieces of student writing may only remain as drafts for various reasons: practice of a new genre or strategy, entry in a person journal, not enough time for revision, and so forth. As students receive instruction in editing, combined with writing strategies, they will create more first drafts that are worthy of revision and bringing to final copy.

To help students understand the components of editing, set up a Taxonomy chart that students can add to as they learn new terms. Post this Taxonomy and have the students keep one in their notebooks. Then expand upon those aspects of editing that require extended instruction and bring about significant writing improvement.

HOW DO WE DO IT?

From Draft to Final Copy—Recognition of the Four Improvers

For persons schooled before the advent of the writing process, the red pen was the symbol of every English teacher. Students handed in papers in black and blue ink and got them back marked in red, often with coded abbreviations such as punc., inc., org., W.W., sp., and others that informed them that their writing was below standard. The teacher was the sole arbiter of what was good writing and what needed serious rewriting. Students often received two grades—one for content (having something worthwhile to say) and the other for grammar (lack of split infinitives, verb disagreements, and other substandard speech forms such as "me and my friend"). Very good writers got A/A, mediocre writers got B/B, and some writers (such as one of the authors of this book) got D/A—nothing of interest in the content but said with perfect grammar and impeccable spelling.

Writers can learn how to improve their writing by focusing on what are called writing improvers:

- Adding significant information or ideas
- Deleting redundant or insignificant information
- Substituting weak or repetitive words
- Moving or rearranging misplaced or poorly sequenced phrases or sentences

These writing improvers provide a teaching methodology for helping students learn to edit in contrast to depending upon the teacher as the "corrector" of all that was wrong. First, teachers can provide students with writing activities in which they add, delete, substitute, and move information. Next, they can clue students as to how they could improve their draft copies with questions relating to each improver.

- What words can you add to make your writing more interesting, vivid, or exciting?
- What information can you add to help your audience know more about what you want to say?
- What punctuation do you need to add to avoid writing two sentences as one sentence?
- Are there commas or question marks or other punctuation marks you need to add?
- What words or statements have you repeated that you can delete or take out of your writing?
- Have you used *and then* more than once or used too many *ands*? Which of these repeated words can you delete?
- Do you need to delete punctuation marks that make your sentences not complete or finished?
- What plain, boring, unexciting adjectives have you used that you can substitute with more vivid, meaningful words?
- What transition words can you use to substitute for *first, second,* or *finally,* or for "*and then*"?
- What verbs can you substitute for verbs such as *go, get, run, walk, say,* and others to make your audience want to read more of your writing?

TAXONOMY SHEET
Transition Words for Guiding Your Audience

Use these words when you need to guide your audience through your writing. For practice, revise one of your previous writings and add any of these words that will make your writing clearer to your readers. Then continue to use these words in your new writings.

A	as soon as, although, above all
B	by and by
C	consequently
D	during, despite
E	eventually
F	frequently, furthermore, first, finally, following that
G	generally
H	however
I	immediately, in addition
J	
K	
L	lately, last
M	meanwhile, moreover, most important
N	nevertheless, naturally
O	often, occasionally, otherwise
P	perhaps
Q	
R	rarely
S	suddenly, since, scarcely, similarly, second
T	therefore, though
U	usually
V	
W	while
X	
Y	yet
Z	

Figure 14.2

■ What lowercase letters need to be substituted with capital letters?

■ What periods need to be substituted with question marks? What commas need to be substituted with periods?

■ What words, phrases, or sentences do you need to move to make your writing more understandable to your audience?

■ Can you move any –ly adverbs to the beginning of your sentences or before the verb for sentence variety?

■ Have you told your story in the right sequence or do you need to move any events from one part of the story to another?

If students have systematically developed Taxonomies and have used Defining Format, Framed Outlines, Profiles, and Three Reasons Why for organizing their writing, they will easily recognize their editing needs and understand how to apply the improvers when they are ready to edit. Posting charts that give a quick overview of writing tips or ways to refine writing provides a guide to students for their own writing and for serving as a peer editor to their classmates.

Using Transitions

Organizational formats and transitions are essential tools that give the audience the road map to the writer's paths. So again, teachers want to provide the students with Taxonomy of transition words that prompt and remind the students of their importance.

Use an arrangement of transition words to move from one paragraph to the next. Figure 14.2 can be posted as a chart or provided to students.

In the following writing sample, the writer used the strategy Composing with Keywords to show the use of transition words. Asking students to compose their own "transition words" paragraphs or stories helps them to realize the value of these words.

Polly Parrot was hungry and very upset with Ms. M. for not feeding her. **However,** Polly loved Ms. M. and **naturally** hoped that her owner was not ill. **From time to time,** Polly tried to call out to Ms.

M., but with no success. **Suddenly,** Polly had an idea. "**Although** she's the one who should feed me, **perhaps** I should be the one to prepare dinner. **Moreover,** Ms. M. may have missed her train. **In the meantime,** I'll set the table. **Since** we usually eat at six o'clock, I'll start cooking shortly."

Scarcely had this thought crossed Polly's mind, when Ms. M. burst into the kitchen full of apologies. "My darling Polly," she pleaded. "Please forgive me. **Despite** what you may have been thinking, I have not forgotten you. **Generally** I leave you something to eat, but today I decided to walk home and I forgot the time."

Rarely was Polly upset with Ms. M., but this indeed was a weak excuse. **Nevertheless,** Polly accepted the apologies. **Otherwise,** she would have to face a sullen owner and an angry mealtime. "I forgive you Ms. M and, **hopefully,** we can enjoy the meal I've prepared for you. " **Fortunately,** Ms. M. remained in good spirits. **As soon as** dinner was ready, Polly Parrot and Ms. M. quietly sat down at the table and ate their meal. **Eventually,** each one forgot any bad feelings and enjoyed the rest of the evening.

Peer and Self-Editing

Every writer must learn to self-edit. Yet, at the same time, the writer needs a peer, a person willing to read or listen to the writing and address the writer's concerns. The peer editor must also respond gently, with just enough judgment or ideas to encourage the writer to continue writing and make the necessary changes. These are mature behaviors that teachers themselves often haven't practiced. However, these behaviors can be taught and learned.

Hopefully, teachers have guided their students through the strategies for writing, and the students have an understanding of what is "good" writing for the genre or topic you have assigned. Students should have skipped lines or doubled spaced on their draft copy.

For the first step of peer editing, pair any two students together, regardless of their writing ability. Each student serves merely as the listener to the other and will read aloud his or her writing to the peer. Instruct the listener, at first, to listen to the whole piece of writing and suggest one word, phrase, or idea to be added. The suggestion can be as simple as "I would like you to add your friend's name in the first sentence." Or, "I think you should add the color of the shoes the elf wore." Tell the students they will add their words by inserting a *caret mark* (^) and then write the word or words. They are not to erase any of the original words but can cross out words if the are making a change. Erasing obliterates any possibility of returning to the original, which writers often want to do or consider. Erasing also is a terrible time waster for students and makes them forget what they wanted to change to. Encourage each student to add at least one item to the writing.

Continue this process of peer reading aloud to the peer, taking the students through each improver. After practicing adding, for example, the students might listen for words that their peers have repeated or overused. With their writing implement, they cross out the overused or excessive words. Again, with the class, discuss words that were deleted. Move through the steps of substituting better words using posted Taxonomies and published thesauruses. Repeat the steps of adding, deleting, and substituting several times before explaining moving since this last improver is generally more difficult for inexperienced writers or "editors."

Peer Review

Many teachers report that they have asked students to read other students' writing with very poor results. The student readers often "can't find anything wrong" with the writing except an occasional spelling or punctuation mistake. This isn't surprising because without direct instruction in peer review, students generally don't know what the reviewer is to look for.

A simple strategy for introducing students to peer reviewing is to provide students with stick-on squares or rectangles that they can use to write suggestions or comments and post on another student's paper. Neither a peer editor nor any other editor ever writes directly on a writer's paper. This is a serious breach of editorial ethics. Tell the students that they are moving from being listening editors to being peer (equal) reading editors. They will carefully read their partner's writing and write their suggestions for adding, deleting, substituting, or moving on a stick-on note and put it on the side of the paper near the words that need changing or fixing. Suggestions on the stick-on paper might look something like these:

- Add *when* you went
- Take out the words *and so*
- Change the word *nice*
- Move the words *last night* to the front of the sentence
- Use a capital letter
- Change the period to a question mark
- Add a *p* to hoping
- Add more about how you felt

- Delete this line that you said before
- Substitute a word like cheerful for happy
- Move the fifth sentence to the end of the paragraph

Teacher Editing

When students learn how to edit their own work and use peer editing to improve their writing, the teacher becomes more of an adviser on aspects of editing that are not yet within the maturity of his or her students. For example, the teacher may need to explain formal versus informal word usage. Students who begin sentences with *"Me and my friend"* need to know that written language requires *"My friend and I."* Mistakes in agreement— *"She don't need so much"*—generally come from the student's natural speech dialect and can be discussed in lessons on dialects or in a private conference with the individual student. From the Taxonomy for Editors and Editing, the following suggestions are offered, which will hopefully make the task of editing easier for the teacher and more beneficial for students.

- *Audience:* Before your students start to write, ask them to imagine who they are writing to and to write who their audience is in the top margin of their draft copy (e.g., my classmates).

- *Consistent Point of View:* Either with a small conference group or with the whole class, point out to the students that the audience must know "where the writer stands" on an issue or idea. Is the writer for or against? Does the writer like or dislike? Does the writer want or not want? If the writer wants to show "the other" side, does she clue the audience?

- *Length:* Writing has length. Short stories are shorter than novels. Haikus are shorter than epics. A research paper is longer than an abstract, but rarely longer than a short book. The length of a writing assignment is important because of the relationship of length to genre. Students are generally graded on appropriate length and, therefore, they need to know length requirements before they can begin to plan their writing.

- *Theme:* The theme is the unifying or dominant idea of a piece of writing and the audience or reader should easily recognize the theme and be able to state it in his or her own words. Students can check if they have written a clear theme by asking three or four of their peers to write their understanding of the theme in one sentence. Be sure to give examples of themes from both literature and factual writing. For example, the theme of *Charlotte's Web* is of the need for friendship, cooperation, and caring among humans and animals. Students who have had consistent practice in writing Premises will be able to state themes and more easily develop their own themes.

- *Voice:* This is the "sound" of the writer—friendly, formal, advisory, admonishing, angry, mature, young, and so forth. The writer must take on a persona—*I am writing as your friend. I am writing as your parent. I am writing as your mentor or teacher.* Voice is related to audience. Therefore, the student writer must match her or his voice to the intended audience, much like giving a talk or speech.

Rubrics

Many local and state assessment requirements use rubrics for writing. *The Random House Unabridged Dictionary* defines a rubric as "any established conduct or procedure." As applied to the assessment of writing, rubrics can be used to reflect the basic benchmarks or established rules of writing as contrasted to speech or conversation. Following are standards to be used in written communications that can be incorporated into rubrics used to assess student writing:

- Keeps to the topic throughout the whole piece of writing and doesn't slip or slide (as in conversation) to another topic.
- Organizes the ideas in some sequence that the reader can follow or recognize.
- Provides the reader with details or information that make the reader *satisfied and not filled with puzzlement or too many questions.*
- Uses the written conventions of capitalization, punctuation, and spelling.
- Writes in the grammar of standard written English in contrast to the informal grammar of speech.

These basic rubrics, which don't come easily to many students, are the standards for all writing, excepting possibly personal journals and now the new genre of e-mail (see Figures 14.3–14.5). It is essential that teachers discuss these rubrics with their students, have them practice them (hopefully through the strategies this book outlines), and then post them prominently in the classroom. Following are a set of Checklists that teachers can use to guide students in following the "rules" or conventions of writing:

- Rubrics for the draft copy for teacher use in both primary and upper grades.
- Rubrics for revised and edited copy for teacher use in primary and upper grades.

■ Personal checklists for students in primary and upper grades.

To arrive at an improvement score or the difference between the Draft Copy and the Revised Copy, add the "numbers" and subtract the difference. Teachers will be able to motivate their students to revise and edit when they begin to see how changes they make in their writing result in a higher score as well as in a better piece of writing.

Draft Copy Rubrics for Teacher Evaluation of Student Writing—Primary Grades

Scores: 1 2 3 4 (low to high)

Name of Student _____

Title of Writing _____

Genre (Narrative, Biography, Persuasive, etc.) _____

Date _____

	1	2	3	4	N.A.
Wrote on the topic					
Organized logically or sequentially					
Used topic sentence(s)					
Added support sentences					
Included significant details					
Had concluding or summary sentence					
Used varied sentence structure					
Had a variety of words or terms					
Had appropriate length for genre or assignment					
Contained several ideas or items of information					
Used capital letters appropriately					
Put in appropriate punctuation					
Spelled conventionally					
Potential for revision towards excellent					

Comments

Figure 14.3

Revised and Edited Copy Rubrics for Teacher Evaluation of Student Writing— Primary Grades

Scores: 1 2 3 4 (low to high)

Name of Student _____

Title of Writing _____

Genre (Narrative, Biography, Persuasive, etc.) _____

Date _____

	1	2	3	4	N.A.
Wrote on the topic					
Organized logically or sequentially					
Used topic sentence(s)					
Added support sentences					
Included significant details					
Had concluding or summary sentence					
Used varied sentence structure					
Had a variety of words or terms					
Had appropriate length for genre or assignment					
Contained several ideas or items of information					
Used capital letters appropriately					
Put in appropriate punctuation					
Spelled conventionally					

Comments

Figure 14.4

Provide students with Figure 14.4 or 14.5 depending on their grade to help improve their draft copy. When they submit their revised copy, they should also submit the completed checklist indicating the improvements they made.

Draft Copy Rubrics for Teacher Evaluation of Student Writing—Grades Four through Twelve

Scores: 1 2 3 4 (low to high)

Name of Student _____

Title of Writing _____

Genre (Narrative, Biography, Persuasive, etc.) _____

Date _____

	1	2	3	4	N.A.
Wrote on the topic					
Organized logically or sequentially					
Had consistent point of view					
Indicated sense of audience					
Used topic sentence(s)					
Added support sentences					
Included significant details					
Had concluding or summary sentence					
Used varied sentence structure					
Had a variety of words or terms					
Used pronouns appropriately					
Used necessary transitional words					
Had appropriate length for genre or assignment					
Contained several ideas or items of information					
Used capital letters appropriately					
Put in appropriate end punctuation					
Used appropriate internal punctuation					
Spelled conventionally					
Potential for revision toward excellent					

Comments

Figure 14.5

SkyLight Professional Development

Revised and Edited Copy Rubrics for Teacher Evaluation of Student Writing—Grades Four through Twelve

Scores: 1 2 3 4 (low to high)

Name of Student _____

Title of Writing _____

Genre (Narrative, Biography, Persuasive, etc.) _____

Date _____

	1	2	3	4	N.A.
Wrote on the topic					
Organized logically or sequentially					
Had consistent point of view					
Indicated sense of audience					
Used topic sentence(s)					
Added support sentences					
Included significant details					
Had concluding or summary sentence					
Used varied sentence structure					
Had a variety of words or terms					
Used pronouns appropriately					
Used necessary transitional words					
Had appropriate length for genre or assignment					
Contained several ideas or items of information					
Used capital letters appropriately					
Put in appropriate end punctuation					
Used appropriate internal punctuation					
Spelled conventionally					

Comments

Figure 14.6

Student Checklist of Improvements

In revising and editing my draft copy, I made the following improvements (if necessary):

Name _____

Title of My Writing _____

Date _____

I revised and edited my paper and made the following improvements:

- Added adjectives
- Substituted (replaced) weak vocabulary
- Combined short, choppy sentences
- Shifted or moved adverbs
- Shifted or moved sentences
- Added missing transitions
- Added missing or significant details or information
- Deleted repetitive words or information
- Corrected errors in punctuation, grammar, and spelling
- Other (please list)

Give these checklists of rubrics to your students for self-evaluation.

Primary Grade Checklist

Name _____

Title of My Writing _____

Genre (Narrative, Biography, Persuasive, etc.) _____

Date _____

I did these revising and editing tasks:	Yes	Not Necessary
Used a Draft Format		
Wrote on the topic		
Wrote as much as I was asked to		
Used topic sentences		
Used support sentences		
Wrote an end or concluding sentence		
Used lots of different words		
I also did these tasks:		
Read my writing aloud to a peer		
Added missing details		
Deleted words I didn't need		
Substituted interesting words for boring words		
Moved any words or sentences that were in the wrong place		
Checked for capital letters		
Checked for punctuation		
Checked my spelling		

Figure 14.7

Checklist for Grades Four through Twelve

Name _____

Title of My Writing _____

Genre (Narrative, Biography, Persuasive, etc.) _____

Date _____

My revising and editing tasks:	Yes	Not Necessary
Used a Draft Format		
Wrote on the topic		
Kept a consistent point of view		
Used the appropriate voice for my audience		
Followed a logical or sequential organization		
Wrote as much as I was asked to		
Used topic sentences		
Used support sentences		
Wrote with sentence variety		
Included necessary transitions		
Included varied vocabulary		
Wrote an end or concluding sentence		
I also did these revising and editing these tasks:		
Read my writing aloud to a peer		
Added missing details		
Deleted words I didn't need		
Substituted interesting or clarifying words		
Moved any words or sentences that were in the wrong place		
Checked for capital letters		
Checked for final and internal punctuation		
Checked and corrected my spelling		

Figure 14.8

LINKING TO THE COMPUTER

The computer—or more appropriately the word processor—truly is the writer's best friend. For many of us, writing by hand or with a typewriter is now unthinkable. People today expect the computer to help add, delete, substitute, and, of course, move and rearrange. Furthermore, they ask it to underline their misspelled words and provide a dictionary to help correct them. They depend on the word processor to remember if they want block paragraphing or indented paragraphing, capital or lower case letters, bullets or numbers. The machine is the guardian editor, although it can easily frustrate them when they choose to write against the conventions and end up with capital letters that they don't want, but the computer insists they must have.

If computers are available to students, teachers should help them learn as much as possible about word processing—from formatting to publishing. Guide them through the menus of *File, Edit, Insert, Format, Tool, Tables,* and *Window* opportunities. Yes, programmed and game activities are fun and may provide instruction, but creativity and thinking develop when your students create their own text—poems, stories, articles—and then enhance their creativity with art forms, fonts, borders, and other "magic" provided by this amazing machine.

CHAPTER 15

Active Learning

A Goal for Every Student

It is only in good writing that you will find how words are best used.

— Jacques Barzun

INTEGRATING WRITING ACROSS THE CURRICULUM

I know about butterflies. A butterfly has six legs and twelve eyes. First the butterfly lays about a hundred eggs and then dies. Then the eggs lay in a warm place for fourteen days till they hatch into larvae. They now eat a lot of food and move on to being a caterpillar. When they get bigger, they turn into a chrysalis. In the chrysalis they turn into a butterfly and when they come out of the chrysalis they are so pretty. That's how much I know about butterflies.

Second grade student

I am a light bulb. I have many pleasures being one. First, I can light up soccer fields at night. While the humans watch, I can watch too. Although the cheers are disruptive, it is still fun to watch the game. Last week I was astounded when one of the teams made five goals in a row.
In addition, I can illuminate an opera house. I love being part of the special effects.
Best of all, I get to help people read. Not only am I doing a great service, but I get to catch up on some great books.
Now you too might want to be an electric light bulb like me.

Fourth grade student

What short answer or worksheet response could match the learning and creativity of expression that are represented in the charming and informative voices of the preceding writers or any of the writers in real classrooms? Writing transforms the student into an active learner—not easily at first, but eventually.

This chapter summarizes what students learn by writing by using a model plan for learning mathematics more thoroughly and effectively through the twelve writing strategies presented in this book. Mathematics is chosen specifically to show how the learning of any subject is better served with the integration of strategy-based writing instruction. Teachers may certainly substitute their own subject areas, but include *all* the strategies.

Figure 15.1 shows the Planning Wheel with mathematics as the focus.

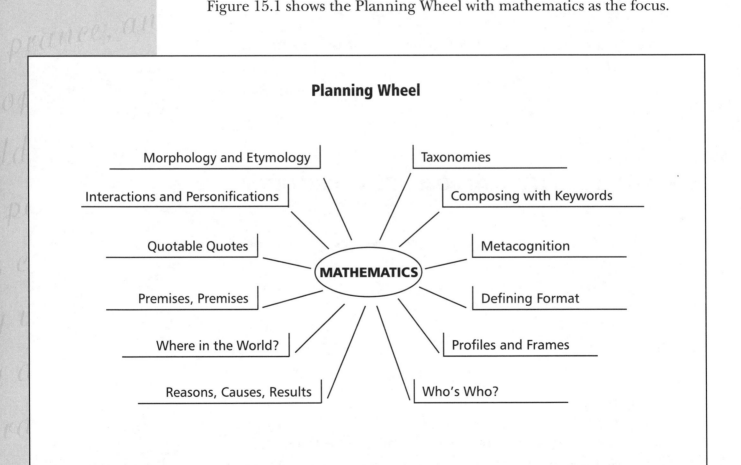

Planning Wheel

Morphology and Etymology

Interactions and Personifications

Quotable Quotes

Premises, Premises

Where in the World?

Reasons, Causes, Results

MATHEMATICS

Taxonomies

Composing with Keywords

Metacognition

Defining Format

Profiles and Frames

Who's Who?

Figure 15.1

STRATEGIES FOR INTEGRATING MATHEMATICS WITH WRITING—A SAMPLE PLAN FOR TEACHING GEOMETRY

1. Students set up their taxonomies of geometry terms.
2. Pre-Assessment: Students enter all the geometry terms they know prior to the unit.
3. Notetaking: Students add newly introduced terms to their Taxonomies.
4. Post-Assessment: Students apply their knowledge of terms in mathematical problems in written work.
5. Students use terms from the Taxonomy for Composing with Keywords.

Examples

We decided to create a circular garden about ten feet in diameter and place a cylindrical sculpture about five meters high in the center.

The pyramid and the prism are two solid geometric shapes that have been created from the triangle. The pyramid became the Egyptian symbol of its Pharaohs and a lasting memory to their power. The prism is much less noble, but very useful for separating the colors in light.

6. Students define selected terms using Defining Format.

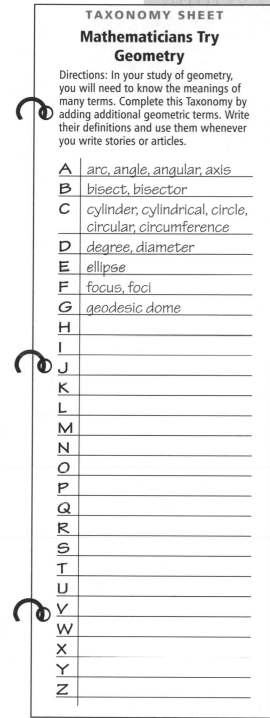

TAXONOMY SHEET
Mathematicians Try Geometry

Directions: In your study of geometry, you will need to know the meanings of many terms. Complete this Taxonomy by adding additional geometric terms. Write their definitions and use them whenever you write stories or articles.

A	arc, angle, angular, axis
B	bisect, bisector
C	cylinder, cylindrical, circle, circular, circumference
D	degree, diameter
E	ellipse
F	focus, foci
G	geodesic dome
H	
I	
J	
K	
L	
M	
N	
O	
P	
Q	
R	
S	
T	
U	
V	
W	
X	
Y	
Z	

Figure 15.2

DEFINING FORMAT

What is a Geodesic Dome?

Question	Category	Characteristics
What is a geodesic dome? A geodesic dome is a	structure that	1. combines the properties of a tetrahedron and the sphere 2. consists of a grid of compression or tension members lying upon or parallel to great circles running in three directions 3. was developed by the architect R. Buckminster Fuller

Figure 15.3

7. Students compose Metacognitive Statements indicating their knowledge of newly learned terms.

Example

As a result of constructing different kinds of triangles in class yesterday, I now understand more about the hypotenuse. I know it is the side of a triangle opposite the right angle. I also learned that the Greek mathematician Pythagoras figured out how to measure the sum of the sides of the square that lie on the hypotenuse. In this great mathematical discovery, Pythagoras stated that the square of the hypotenuse of a right triangle is equal to the sum of the squares on the other two sides.

8. Students use a Frame or Profile to expand upon information related to one of the terms.

Example

Profile of a Polygon
Name of Polygon—Parallelogram
Number of Sides—four
Number of Angles—4
Total Degrees of Angle—360
Other Name or Category—Type of Quadrilateral
Other Quadrilaterals—Square, Rectangle, Rhombus
Distinguishing Characteristic—Parallelogram has two obtuse angles and two acute angles.*

A square has four equal sides and four right angles. A rectangle has opposite sides of equal length and four right angles. Rhombus has four equal sides, but no right angles.

Measurement Formula—The area is the product of the base x the height. To get the perimeter, we add the length of all four sides.

*Other Information—Note that a parallelogram can also be a square, rectangle, or rhombus because the sides of these polygons are parallel. A parallelogram is a plane figure, but it can be made into a three-dimensional figure called a parallelepiped.

9. Student selects one or more prominent mathematicians from the Taxonomy Who's Who in Mathematics and writes a Biographical Sketch focusing on the person's contributions and accomplishments.

Example

Lise Meitner was an Austrian physicist and mathematician who worked with the German physical chemist Otto Hahn and helped discover the element protactinium in 1918. In addition, she was a professor of physics at the University of Berlin from 1926 to 1933, but was forced to leave Germany in 1938. She continued her work at the University of Stockholm where she published her first paper on nuclear fission and atomic theory. Later in her life she came to America and was a visiting professor at Catholic University in Washington, DC and lecturer in physics and mathematics in 1946 at Bryn Mawr College.

TAXONOMY SHEET

Taxonomy of Geographer's Measurements

Below are words that represent measurement related to geography and the work of geographers. Check in your mathematics book or other resource to find what they equal or how they are measured or used.

A	area, acre, arc
B	boundary
C	circumference
D	degrees, density
E	equator, equinox, elevation
F	
G	Greenwich mean time
H	hemisphere
I	International date line
J	
K	kilometer
L	longitude, latitude
M	meter, meridian, mile
N	
O	orbit
P	population
Q	
R	
S	solstice, scale, sphere
T	
U	
V	
W	
X	
Y	yard
Z	

Figure 15.4

10. Student researches or studies aspects of mathematics that relate to geography as part of the strategy Where in the World. One activity might be to create a Taxonomy of Mathematical Terms Needed by Geographers. Another possibility is to research mathematics among early peoples in different parts of the world (e.g., Mayans, Arabs, Chinese). Figure 15.4 shows a Taxonomy of Geographer's Measurements prepared by a group of middle school students.

11. Students write an essay or essays relating to mathematics using personal, persuasive, or explanatory writing. Following are sample topics:

Personal

– There are three reasons why I need to learn mathematics.

– There are three ways that I use mathematics in my life.

– By studying mathematics, I will have opportunities in several high-paying careers.

Persuasive

– We should encourage girls, as well as boys, to study advanced mathematics for these reasons.

– All students in America need to do well in mathematics for these reasons.

– There are three reasons why American students need to improve their mathematical skills in a global economy.

Explanatory

– There are three ways to get better grades in mathematics.

– Albert Einstein (or another mathematician) contributed three important mathematical ideas to society.

– Astronomers (or other professionals) use mathematics in several important (or significant) ways.

12. Students read a book or story in which mathematics is important or prominent. They then write the Premise of the book as it relates to mathematics or write about an aspect or scene from the book that deals with mathematics. Here are several stories or books that can be used for this activity.

   • *The Phantom Tollbooth* by Norton Juster—A major character is the Dodecahedron, a twelve-sided figure, who is in conflict with the Mathemagician over how to protect the city of Digitopolis in its dispute with the city of Dictionopolis.

   • *Through the Looking Glass* by Lewis Carroll—Humpty Dumpty tries to convince Alice that we are better off celebrating un-birthdays since we have three hundred sixty-four of them.

   • *The Clan of the Cave Bear* by Jean M. Auel—A superb novel for upper high school students, it gives the story of Ayla, an outsider to the clan and a female, who learns her first lesson in mathematics from Creb, the clan's magician, and then quickly goes on to surpass his knowledge.

   Of course, there are numerous counting books for young students and more advanced books on numbers and related information for older students. Librarians and the Internet are excellent sources for identifying these books.

13. Students begin to make a collection of Quotable Quotes related to numbers and other mathematical ideas and then formulate their own quotable quotes.

   Examples

   "Mathematics, rightly viewed, possesses not only truth, but supreme beauty—a beauty cold and austere, like that of sculpture."
   Bertrand Russell in Mysticism and Logic *(1918)*

   "All things begin in order, so shall they end, and so shall they begin again; according to the ordainer of order and mystical mathematics of the city of heaven."
   Sir Thomas Browne (1605–1682)

   "Angling [fishing] may be said to be so like mathematics, that it can never be fully learnt."
   Izaak Walton in The Compleat Angler *(1653)*

"...one of the nicest things about mathematics...is that many of the things which can never be, often are...it's very much like your trying to reach Infinity. You know it's there, but you just don't know where."

The .58 Child in the Phantom Tollbooth

14. Students assume the persona of a mathematical concept or figure and write to another mathematical concept or figure, as in the following example of a triangle writing to a rectangle.

Dr. B. A Triangle
3 Scalene Lane
Isosceles, CA 33333

U. R. Square, Ph.D.
4 Right Angle Terrace
Straightville, WY 44444

Dear Dr. Square,

I was delighted to hear that you are doing research on triangles and want a full description of my family and its accomplishments. First, you should know that all Triangles have three sides connected with three angles equaling 180 degrees. You will notice this is in contrast to your family which always has 360 degrees. However, we have the distinct advantage of having obtuse, acute, or right angles and are not limited, as you are, to only right angles. Furthermore, we can choose to be Isosceles, Equilateral, or Scalene depending on the similarity or dissimilarity of our sides and angles, allowing us to have our own unique look. Finally, we have become immortalized as the basis for the three-dimensional figure known as the pyramid.

I trust this information is what you are seeking. If you need additional details, please feel free to contact me. I am available by phone every third day or you can e-mail me at Triangle.com.

Very sincerely,
Beter A. Triangle.

15. Student studies Morphology and Etymology of mathematical terms and creates an *A to Z* book or other reference materials. The three examples here are from a sixth grade student's book titled *Mathematical Etymologies from A to Z*, which the student adapted from *Dictionary of Word Origins* (1990) and *Word Mysteries and Histories* (1986).

> Abacus—a counting device for adding and subtracting. The word abacus comes from the Hebrew word abaq, which means "dust." The Greeks then borrowed this word to describe a board covered with dust or sand that they could draw on. Then this Greek word began to mean "table." Later on the word was used in Latin and changed to the Latin form "abacus." In the fourteenth century, English speakers began to use abacus to mean a counting frame with movable balls.

> Number—a symbol to show quantity or amount. Etymologists think that this word came from the Greek word nemein, which meant to distribute. Then it moved into Latin as the word numerus. Eventually, the French borrowed the word, calling it nombre. When William the Conqueror came to England from Normandy, he introduced this word and the English pronounced it "number." Other words then grew from this word such as numeral, numerator, numerical, numerous, and enumerate.

> Zero—a symbol to mark place value or the absence of quantity. This word comes from the Arab word sift, which originally meant to cipher or write. The Italian traders a few hundred years before Marco Polo changed the word to zefiro. A few hundred years later, the French traders called this word cipher, which they had borrowed from the Latin cifra. By the late Middle Ages, English had two words from this one word—cipher and zero.

LINKING TO THE COMPUTER

The world of mathematics is truly enhanced by one's computer knowledge. Computer knowledge broadens understanding of mathematics as well as of other subjects. Students can access sites on the Internet that relate to any topic. In the subject of mathematics, there are sites that offer mathematical games, mathematical activities, problems, brain teasers, weekly challenges, logic puzzles, activities, and exercises.

Many students have already discovered for themselves the vast world of cyberspace. The school's task is to guide students to those sites on the Internet that can provide them with the same mind-expanding experiences that young people a millennium ago had when they took books out from the public library, which allowed them to step into a world beyond their neighborhoods or villages. Now of course, with Web sites and e-mail (and who knows what else is to come) students only need to know how to ask the right questions and then push the buttons for the answers. The greater challenge will be whether students will be able to reconstruct the answers in their own words, so that they, in turn, can pass on new information to an enormous world that sits within the computer on their desks. Perhaps some of the writing strategies in this book will be of assistance in this exciting task.

Bibliography

Andersen, Hans Christian. 1993. *The Complete Hans Christian Andersen Fairy Tales*. New York: Grammercy.

Auel, Jean M. 1980. *Clan of the Cave Bear*. New York: Crown.

Aton, John. 1990. *Dictionary of Word Origins*. New York: Little, Brown & Company.

Atwell, Nancy 1998. 2d ed. *In the Middle: New Understandings about Writing, Reading, and Learning*. New York: Greenwood-Heinemann.

Beck, Isabel L. et al. 1989. *Seascapes*. Orlando, FL: Harcourt, Brace & Co.

Bereiter, Carl, and M. Scardamalia. 1985. Cognitive Coping Strategies and the Problem of Inert Knowledge. In *Thinking and Learning Skills, vol. 2, Current Research and Open Questions,* edited by S. C. Chipman, J. W. Segal, and R. Glazers. Hillsdale, NJ: Erlbaum.

Bettelheim, Bruno. 1975. *The Uses of Enchantment*. New York: Random.

Brenner, Barbara. 1993. *Wagon Wheels*. New York: HarperCollins.

Bryson, Bill. 1990. *The Mother Tongue: English and How It Got That Way*. New York: William Morrow.

Caine, Renate Nummela, and Geoffrey Caine. 1991. *Teaching and the Human Brain*. Alexandria, VA: Association for Supervision and Curriculum Development.

Carroll, Lewis. 1965. *Through the Looking-Glass*. New York: Random House.

Claiborne, Robert. 1983. *Our Marvelous English Tongue: The Life and Times of the English Language*. New York: Times Books.

Christelow, Ellen. 1998. *Five Little Monkeys Jumping on the Bed.* New York: Clarion Books.

Costa, Arthur L. 1991. *The School as a Home for the Mind.* Palatine, IL.: Skylight Publishing.

Editors of the American Heritage Dictionary. 1986. *Word Mysteries and Histories.* Boston: Houghton Mifflin.

Einstein, Albert. 1954. *Ideas and Opinions.* New York: Bonanza Books.

Feuerstein, Reuven, et al. 1997. Process as Content in Education of Exceptional Children. In *Supporting the Spirit of Learning: When Process Is Content,* edited by Arthur L. Costa and Rosemarie M. Liebman. Thousand Oaks, CA.: Corwin Press.

Gardner, Howard. 1983. *Frames of Mind.* New York: Basic Books.

Gardner, Howard. 1993. *Multiple Intelligences.* New York: Basic Books.

Hirsch, E. D. Jr. 1987. *Cultural Literacy: What Every American Needs to Know.* Boston: Houghton Mifflin.

Hyerle, David. 1995. *Thinking Maps: Tools for Learning.* Cary, NC: Innovative Sciences.

Juster, Norton. 1989. *The Phantom Tollbooth.* New York: Random House.

Kennedy, Colleen. 1996. Teaching Discourse through Writing. In *Developing Verbal Talent,* VanTasssel-Baska, ed. New York: Allyn and Bacon.

Lowry, Lois. 1989. *Number the Stars.* New York: Dell.

Martin, Bill. 1991. *Brown Bear, Brown Bear, What Do You See?* New York: Holt, Rinehart and Winston.

McCrum, Robert, William Cran, and Robert MacNeil. 1986. *The Story of English.* New York: Viking.

Milne, A. A. 1957. *The Complete Collection of Winnie the Pooh.* New York: Penguin Books.

Oxford Dictionary of Quotations. 1980. 3rd. ed. New York: Oxford University Press.

Ogle, Donna. 1986. K-W-L: A Teaching model that develops active reading of expository text. *The Reading Teacher* 39: 564-571.

Paola, Tomie di. 1992. *Strega nona.* New York: Simon & Schuster

Paulsen, Gary. 1987. *Hatchet.* New York: Simon & Schuster.

Perkins, David. 1992. *Smart Schools.* New York: Free Press.

Potter, Beatrix. 1909. *The Tale of Petter Rabbit.* New York: Frederick Warne & Company.

Schlein, Miriam. 1966. *The Way Mothers Are.* Chicago, IL: Albert Whitman Publishing.

Sklar, Daniel Judah. 1991. *Playmaking: Children Writing and Performing Their Own* Plays. New York: Teachers & Writers Collaborative.

Smith, Frank. 1982. *Writing and the Writer.* New York: Holt, Rinehart and Winston.

Spivey, Nancy Nelson. 1996. Reading, writing, and the construction of meaning. In *Developing Verbal Talent,* New York: Allyn and Bacon.

Steckler, Arthur. 1979. *101 Words and How They Began.* Garden City, NY: Doubleday & Company.

VanTassel-Baska, Joyce. 1996. *Developing Verbal Talent.* New York: Allyn and Bacon.

Vygotsky, Lev. 1962. *Thought and Language.* Cambridge, MA: MIT Press.

Zindel, Paul. 1978. *The Pigman.* New York: Harper & Row.

Zinsser, William. 1980. *On Writing Well,* 2d ed. New York: Harper & Row.

Index

**CORWIN
PRESS**

The Corwin Press logo—a raven striding across an open book—represents the union of courage and learning. Corwin Press is committed to improving education for all learners by publishing books and other professional development resources for those serving the field of K–12 education. By providing practical, hands-on materials, Corwin Press continues to carry out the promise of its motto: **"Helping Educators Do Their Work Better."**